Beyond Loss

LILLY SINGER,
Director, Bereavement Center, Westchester Jewish Community Services

MARGARET SIROT,
& SUSAN RODD

Beyond Loss

A PRACTICAL GUIDE THROUGH GRIEF TO A MEANINGFUL LIFE

E. P. DUTTON NEW YORK

Published in the United States by E. P. Dutton, a division of NAL Penguin Inc., 2 Park Avenue, New York, N.Y. 10016.

Published simultaneously in Canada by
Fitzhenry and Whiteside, Limited, Toronto.

Library of Congress Cataloging-in-Publication Data
Singer, Lilly.
  Beyond loss: a practical guide through grief to a meaningful life /
Lilly Singer, Margaret Sirot, and Susan Rodd. — 1st ed.
    p. cm.
  ISBN 0-525-24707-6
  1. Widows—United States—Life skills guides. 2. Widowers—United
States—Life skills guides. 3. Grief. I. Sirot, Margaret.
II. Rodd, Susan. III. Title.
HQ1058.5.U5S58 1988
640.24'0654—dc 19   88-14882
                      CIP

Designed by David Lui

10 9 8 7 6 5 4 3 2 1

First Edition

Grateful acknowledgment is given for permission to quote excerpts from the following works:

A Death in the Family by James Agee. Copyright © 1957 by the James Agee Trust. Reprinted by permission of Grosset and Dunlap, Inc.

A Guide Through Grief by Roberta Temes. Copyright © 1977 by Mandala. Reprinted by permission of Irvington Publishers, Inc.

A Grief Observed by C. S. Lewis. Copyright © 1961 by N. W. Clark, afterword © 1976 by Chad Walsh. Reprinted by permission of Harper & Row Publishers, Inc.

Diaries of Anaïs Nin by Anaïs Nin. Copyright © 1966 by Anaïs Nin. Reprinted by permission of Harcourt Brace Jovanovich, Inc.

"Mourning: New Studies Affirm Its Benefits" by Daniel Goleman, The New York Times. Copyright © 1985 by The New York Times Company. Reprinted by permission.

On Death and Dying by Elisabeth Kübler-Ross. Copyright © 1969 by Elisabeth Kübler-Ross. Reprinted by permission of Macmillan Publishing Company, a division of Macmillan, Inc.

Acknowledgments

Thanks to the following for their contributions to this book:

Dorrie Rosen Associates, Verona, New Jersey; Barbara Quint Associates, Inc., White Plains, New York; Robert B. Schlather; Mary Ellen Fenner; Bruce Eamons; Lieutenant John Gendall, Greenwich, Connecticut, Police; Mildred Galef, CSW, director of Community Education, Westchester Jewish Community Services; Waldo Jones, headmistress, Lower School, Rippowam-Cisqua, Bedford, New York; Nina Evans, M.D., medical director, Westchester Jewish Community Services; Sherry Birnbaum, assistant director of the Bereavement Center, Westchester Jewish Community Services; Ilise Gold, career and life planning specialist, Westport, Connecticut; Dr. Edith Beck.

We also wish to thank all the widows and widowers who were kind enough to endure probing questions and painful recollections in an effort to help other bereaved people. You have made a generous contribution.

Contents

CONTENTS

Foreword

This is a book about hope and personal growth after the loss of a spouse. It provides very practical advice that can be quickly put to work: specific solutions to the difficulties confronting survivors, assurances that time is only one of the healing factors. At a time of loss, survivors need help and support. Here is a book that offers it—to widows, to widowers, to grief-stricken families, and to those anxious to help them.

Lilly Singer is director of the Bereavement Center of Westchester Jewish Community Services (WJCS), a nonsectarian organization. The Bereavement Center is one of the finest and most comprehensive in the United States. The collaboration of this fine agency and this extraordinary woman has created a unique program that answered an enormous need. Combining her life experiences, her educational background, and the support and encouragement of WJCS, Mrs. Singer's program has received national and international acclaim. Mrs. Singer is constantly sought as a consultant to mental health care and religious groups. Her intuitiveness, her connectedness, and her understanding give Mrs. Singer the ability to make this important professional contribution.

Forced by World War II to leave Poland with her family, Mrs. Singer lived in several countries before she arrived in the United States. While working toward a medical degree, she met and married her husband, Ernest. She resumed her studies part-time, concentrating on psychology, after her two children entered school. When her husband died unexpectedly of a heart attack at age fifty-four, the encouragement of family and friends supported her decision to complete her training.

Westchester Jewish Community Services offered Mrs. Singer the opportunity to develop and lead a group for widows and widowers who needed therapeutic and emotional support as well as a social network. This work expanded rapidly, and soon Mrs. Singer had added a group for children, groups for parents of school-aged children, groups for the newly widowed, and groups for people ready to go on with their lives. The impact was tremendous, and word of it spread throughout the mental health care community and beyond.

Mrs. Singer has made an enormous difference to the thousands of people with whom she has had contact, from the professionals who have adapted her model to uncounted groups who have seen her at national and international conferences, heard her on radio and television, and read her articles.

This book focuses on the issues of the grief-stricken family, from the end of the funeral until the family and its members are ready to leave bereavement behind and learn to use the memory of their loved one as a constructive and energizing force in their daily lives. There are no "silver linings" in this book, but there are survival techniques, acknowledgments of common needs, examples of many individuals across a spectrum of ages and situations who not only "endured, but prevailed."* It is this wisdom of experience, culled from years of work in the field, that Lilly Singer presents here.

LEONARD ROHMER
Executive Director
Westchester Jewish Community Service
1957–81

*William Faulkner, Nobel Prize acceptance speech, 1949.

Introduction

Egyptian mythology records the strange tale of a bird of rare beauty called the phoenix. The phoenix, it is said, lives for five or six hundred years and then consumes itself by fire. But the tale doesn't end there. Transcending death, the phoenix rises from its ashes, thus beginning its long cycle of life all over again.

In many ways, this book resembles the rebirth of the phoenix and its flight into a newfound existence. Although it begins with death, it has a happy ending. But, as with the phoenix, that ending is just its beginning.

It is the story of our own lives, and those of many others, who have experienced the loss of a mate and not only have lived to tell the tale but have traveled beyond the days of loss into new understandings of life and new purposes within it. It is the story too of those who helped us find the way—the friends, relatives, and mentors who said or did the right thing at the right time and never gave up on us. These staunch supporters can never be adequately repaid. But their gifts of understanding and compassion can be passed along to others in need.

And so, with gratitude and love for those who gave so much of themselves, and with compassion and understanding for those who are newcomers to grief, this book is our effort to take all we have learned through our days of loss and pass it on.

Here then, in her words, is the story of how this book began for Susan.

Our twin daughters were just seven weeks old; our older girls were seven, five, and three. Twins had not been expected and were, we thought then, the surprise of a lifetime. Finding ourselves in the startling but joyful situation of suddenly having five daughters and only one bathroom, we were in the process of enlarging our home. I wanted it to include an old-fashioned front porch, for in my mind I held a picture of a day, still far ahead of us, when Joe and I would sit together rocking on the front porch, awaiting the arrival of our children, who would, of course, bring their children to visit us.

It was the picture of a day that would never come to be. For, on a quite ordinary and taken-for-granted afternoon, a bigger surprise, terrifying and shattering, opened our front door and entered our lives forever. It eradicated the rocking chairs, and ultimately left both the addition and the family incomplete. As I visited with a friend, showing off my beautiful babies, Joe came home with the announcement that the strange and growing freckle that had just been surgically removed from his back was malignant.

For the next three years, our lives were filled with days of wild, desperate hopes and days of empty, unremitting despair. The nights were worse. There were bouts with major surgery and long weeks when Joe hung on the critical list as the melanoma spread, first to the lungs, and, finally, to the brain. As I watched my children grow, I watched my husband die. I remember one heartbreaking return from the hospital when Abby, who was then two and a half, turned to her father and said brightly, "You're not going to cry, Dad; you've got new pajamas!" But he did cry.

A few months later, he died of a cerebral hemorrhage. Our oldest daughter was ten; the twins were three.

The remaining family floundered. After the first terrible Christmas without him, our leaching fields failed (our kitchen sink failed right along with them), and, as new ones could not be dug until spring, we washed our dishes in the bathtub all winter. One neighbor was discovered stealing our firewood. Another sent our dog to the pound.

Wretched, we drew into ourselves, apart from the world and from each other. Needing to cling to something, I chose my piano, shutting out the rest of life with the sounds of practicing. But even the music could not drown out the truth; my children had a zombie for a mother.

Somehow—although we had no techniques for survival—we survived. In spite of ourselves, we changed and grew. When the life insurance ran out and there was no more money to pay the taxes on the house, I sold the home of my marriage. It turned out to be a healthy move. Then the hours of desperate practicing led to a challenging job with a music magazine. The family began to grow back together again.

It was nine years later, in a new town, when I had a new life and hopes, once again, for the future, that a man at a dinner party, on hearing that I was a widow, said, "You must meet my friend Margaret Sirot."

And here, in Margaret's words, is the description of the loss and subsequent healing process that would one day spark the idea of sharing her experience of growth in an effort to help others locked in grief.

I drove even faster than usual that day, trying to get back before Marv did so I could fill him in on the school I had just seen. A silly love song from Flashdance *kept going through my head. I wanted to tell Marv about that too; maybe I had finally come up with "our song," this year's version.*

I picked up one daughter, dropped off another, threw chicken into the oven to barbecue, and dashed upstairs to change into jeans. Our youngest child, Laura, was the only one around when the door-bell rang. Her voice echoed up the stairwell: "Mom, it's a police-man; I think it's serious." Buttoning my shirt, I pranced downstairs, certain that the dog had been found wandering, or something.

As I walked toward the screen door, I could not quite under-stand why the man did not reflect my grin. "Are you Margaret?" he asked. I thought how odd it was that he knew my first name. He asked if he could speak to me alone, but our daughter stayed within hearing distance. His hollow voice continued: "There has been an accident on I-95. A truck has jumped the guardrail and hit a car head-on. Your husband has been killed."

All my muscles seemed to go into spasm for a moment. And then:

"Oh, no, you must be mistaken."

"Was your husband on I-95 this afternoon?"

"He was going to visit his mother, to persuade her to agree to surgery."

But a grisly phone conversation with a hospital emergency room had to take place before I could even believe that it might have happened.

Laura, in the meantime, had hysterically called our dearest neighbors, who were, mercifully, the first to arrive. Then, slowly, I made the calls to family and friends, and they gathered.

My children had to be collected—one from Safe Rides, one from New York, and one from school. An emissary was sent, and each child assumed it was their grandmother who had died, that it was she who was the emergency. But, instead of losing their eighty-five-year-old grandmother, each of the four had to deal with the unfathomable disaster of the sudden loss of their forty-five-year-old father.

"The one thing I know," I told them, "is that we will be okay." They will remember that all their lives, so I'm glad I said it. Had I any idea of what I and they would go through between that night and "okay," I might have given up on the spot.

The grim firsts started almost immediately: my husband's birth-day, our anniversary, more birthdays, Christmas. When the unbear-

*ableness of it didn't lessen, I allowed myself a decision moratorium:
"I will decide whether or not to survive in the spring."*

*It was a hideous winter. I remember three days with no elec-
tricity, water, or heat, car problems, kid problems, dog problems,
and two funerals. On April 28, I got drunk with an old friend and
made the decision to go on with life. (I gave myself another nine-
month moratorium on deciding why.) But by then shock had thawed
to grief, and I was truly despondent. I would get from place to place
and through each situation by asking myself, What is the best thing
that can happen? What is the worst thing that can happen? On
the day that it made absolutely no difference, I knew I had hit
bottom.*

*Although I had never considered a support group during any
other period of my life, I was desperate. At the urging of my oldest
daughter, Ellen, I joined one that was led by a skilled therapist and
fellow widow—someone I could truly respect, and from whom I
could learn much. That is how I met Lilly Singer. This book is how
she helped me heal.*

Please assume that you too are a member of Lilly Singer's
group. Although you will not often hear her voice in the
sense of "Lilly said this," or "Lilly thinks that," what we will
present in these pages is her wisdom, understanding, and
guidance through experiences that, without her insight,
might have remained meaningless, incomprehensible, and
chaotic.

As head of a complex bereavement center, Lilly supports
profoundly wounded individuals through severe traumas of
loss. In time, she helps survivors convert their life-shattering
crises into avenues of growth and further personal development. The aim of this work is to help the bereaved not simply
to return to their previous level of functioning but to surpass
that level and meet successfully the challenges of being
alone.

Lilly assures all who come to her that the very act of
seeking help is the first step in a process that will end well.
Although you, like the many who arrive bereft on her door-

step, may at first view happy ending assurances with great misgivings, take heart. It has ended well for us, and for many others whom you will meet in this book's pages. You, too, have within yourself the power to achieve your own happy ending. You, like the phoenix, can move beyond loss into the hopes and joys of a different life.

Part I

IMMEDIATE
CONCERNS

1 | After the Funeral

There's been a Death, in the Opposite House,
As lately as Today—
I know it, by the numb look
Such Houses have—alway—
—EMILY DICKINSON

*It feels like being mildly drunk, or concussed. There is a sort of
invisible blanket between the world and me. I find it hard to
take in what anyone says. . . .*
—C. S. LEWIS, A GRIEF OBSERVED

*At the first meeting of the support group she
attended shortly after her husband's death, Sally began to talk about
the pills she was methodically saving in order to have enough of them*

to commit suicide. With perfect clarity (and this was the only thing she was clear about), she explained that she had reached this decision when she realized that nothing but the ending of her own life would stop the excruciating pain of her irrevocable loss. She intended to use the pills as soon as she tidied up a few things. There was no one in the room who could not remember having similar feelings.

The death of a spouse is one of the most traumatic experiences most human beings ever face in their lives. It will happen to almost half of those who are married. Unless you are one of the few who die with their spouses—in an automobile accident, for instance, or a plane crash—if you have entered a committed, lasting relationship, you will be either the person who dies first or the survivor, who is left to carry on when so much of the meaning of existence has seemingly been shattered.

An experience this overwhelming and devastating cannot be absorbed in a day, or in a week; often it takes months. The mind's initial reaction to an experience of devastation is shock. This type of shock is described by the dictionary as "(a) something which jars the emotions as if with a violent, unexpected blow; (b) the disturbances of function, equilibrium or mental faculties caused by such a blow."

When Susan's husband died, guests at the gathering that followed the memorial service were amazed at the poise she displayed as she greeted all with a smile and then busily concerned herself with their welfare: Did they have enough to eat? Would they like to see the new, unfinished living room?

A cousin sat silently in a corner with tears and mascara streaming down her face. A co-worker broke down, sobbing openly as he recalled the last days of his friend.

Why was Susan smiling?

"I don't think it could have been a very happy marriage," one guest remarked to another.

An unhappy marriage had nothing to do with it. Susan was operating in a state of shock.

Shock is nature's protection against a reality that is, for a time, too strong, painful, and threatening to be faced. It lasts almost as long as it is needed, serving as a buffer against the feelings of panic that accompany an amputated reality. If you have recently lost your partner, and if you find yourself responding with words and gestures inappropriate to (or in denial of) the situation, the chances are that you are under the protection of shock. You may feel strangely wooden—rather like a dummy in the hands of a ventriloquist. Do not be alarmed. When you are able to begin to face the reality of your loss, your feelings will return.

When they do, be prepared for an onslaught. After the loss of the human being around whom so much of your life was centered, you are apt to awaken (if you have slept) one morning to a flood of terrifying questions: Why should I get out of bed? Who needs me? What can I do to fill this day and make it pass?

Feelings of grief are compounded by the fact that, besides the loss of the person you promised to love and cherish until this moment (which seemed so far off when those vows were exchanged), you are faced with the loss of the role you occupied, often for most of your adult life. And at first the terrible fears—What's going to happen to me? Am I going to be able to manage? and Is it worth it even to try?—override the sorrow. All of grief's complex emotions (denial, anger, guilt) will awaken with your feelings, but the predominant emotion of the moment is fear, and the state in which you move through your days is one of shock.

Whether your spouse's death was anticipated or sudden, the reality that the most significant person in your life is gone, the most important relationship ended, is unbearable. You will feel alternately numb and panicky, withdrawn and needy, entirely reasonable and utterly distraught. Your nerves will behave like incredibly sensitive litmus paper; the slightest internal or external thought or change will register alarmingly. There is an eerie, Alice in Wonderland quality that accompanies this period—with just a dash of the Mad Hatter thrown in for good measure. On most days, you will feel as if you have drunk the shrinking potion causing even life's simplest problems to parade, giantlike, around you. On other days you'll feel yourself to be the giant, distanced by the height of your loss from the human goings-on beneath you.

To this period of uncontrollable feelings and nerve-jangling sensitivity there are as many different reactions as there are individuals. Some sleep more than usual—all day and all night if they can; others, unable to face awakening to the rediscovery of heartbreaking loss, sleep as little as possible. Some read compulsively, vicariously substituting the drama of a protagonist's existence for their own bleak fate. Others find their loss so distracting that they are unable to make sense of even a simple sentence. Many turn to round-the-clock TV watching. (Those of a misery-loves-company frame of mind often find the vicissitudes of the soap opera and the horrors of the daily news strangely comforting.) Some survivors become unpredictably social; they accept all invitations, drop in on friends, and go to the movies, attempting to avoid the echoing loneliness that faces them in the home so recently shared.

All these reactions are both typical and "normal." They are the means by which individuals temporarily distract themselves from pain and loss, thus making it possible to survive another day and night.

There are other reactions that are far more dangerous; they are also very tempting. These include drinking heavily as a means of escape, turning increasingly to a dependence on the tranquilizers the doctor so kindly prescribed for you, smoking marijuana or crack, and using hard drugs.

Keep in mind the fact that there is no formula or timetable for healing, and give the wrenching feelings of loss their space. *Do not try to mask them!* This awful period must be directly experienced. No one can live through it for you. And, if you do not face it now, when the people around you expect it, you most certainly will face it later.

In the absence of a support group, or a trained and sympathetic clergyperson or mental health care professional, a nonjudgmental friend and confidant will be invaluable. In the process of trying to conceptualize the new reality (which you want so much *not* to be real), you will find yourself compulsively repeating the story of your loss to your friend—or, in the best instances, friends. It's a lot of trouble for just one person to handle. For the time being, your friends will have to bear the burden of watching you and listening to you talk, ruminate, remember, and, most of all, cry.

And your friends *will* watch you. In fact, be prepared for careful scrutiny. Slightly nervous, high-pitched comments, such as "My, but you're looking well!" "Are you getting enough sleep?" and an almost overly cheerful "How are you doing?" may make you feel as if you are living in a fishbowl. Actually, these are words of concern from the people who care about you. Try to keep this in mind when you are tempted to make a caustic remark to the third person in a row who comments on the weight you have lost or the dark circles under your eyes.

As a matter of fact, outward appearance often has little to do with inner reality. Some respond to loss with an almost fanatical concern about their looks.

When Margaret's husband died, she became obsessed with good grooming. She found herself visiting the beauty parlor two or three times a week—something she had never done before. Without her husband's reflected approval of her appearance, Margaret needed instant outward reassurance, bought at the beauty parlor, to convince herself that she was "okay"—at least in one way.

This type of behavior belongs to the group of individuals who need to feel in control of their lives. Struck by an uncontrollable blow of fate, they quickly turn their energies to the things they can control. Their makeup is perfect; their socks match their ties.

Others, who adhere in more normal days to a sort of roll-with-the-flow attitude, tend to let their appearances go when under great stress. They gain or lose weight (according to their bent), becoming "too fat" or "too thin," forget haircuts, and dress in whatever happens to be cleanest or closest—whether it matches or becomes them or not.

The same principles apply to the state of their homes. Controllers plunge into housekeeping. (These are the people who, in noncrisis existence, like to vent their anger by cleaning closets.)

Two nights after her husband's death, as friends began to gather in her living room, Ann became acutely distressed when she realized that the cocktail napkins she was distributing did not match her candles. What kind of person could she be, she thought, to be mixing yellow cocktail napkins with blue candles on a night as important as this one? Her daughter, on the other hand, who was a young lady from the roll-with-the-flow school, was horrified to find her mother—just two nights after her husband's death—concerned with such a trivial matter as cocktail napkins.

Regardless of which school you fit into, life will relentlessly march from one day to the next, and as it does you will feel assaulted by the demands that the needs of basic survival make on your energies.

A few weeks into her widowhood, Margaret was undone by a chicken—a roasted one. As she stood at the foot of the table, presiding over the family dinner, she suddenly realized that she didn't know how to carve it. With poultry shears and carving knife in hand, she burst into hysterical tears.

This is the time when all the practical realities of life on your own appear as a monolithic, unapproachable mass. The vague and unsettling urgency of "I have to," regarding both significant and insignificant matters, naggingly prods and pushes the mind. For instance, dispensing with the clothing and possessions of your mate is often an issue that weighs heavily. There are some things that will not wait, but it is essential to separate those that really must be dealt with immediately from those that can be temporarily postponed. (Sorting through your mate's possessions is a job that can be postponed until you are stronger.)

The problems of maintaining a cash flow while you wait for claims to be settled (and they take considerable time) and Social Security benefits to begin (they take time, too) must be resolved. You may have to borrow money to ease this temporary blight. Wills, probate court, death certificates (you'll need many of them), bank and insurance matters must be dealt with in all their complexities. In fact, economic matters are so important, yet often so perplexing, that the solving of

ESSENTIALS AND NONESSENTIALS

	Must Be Given Priority	Can Be Postponed	Should Be Postponed	Should Be Avoided at All Costs
Getting Dressed	✔			
Going to the Beauty Parlor or the Barber		✔		
Making the Beds		✔		
Changing the Sheets Before They Smell	✔			
Serving Well-balanced, Nutritious Meals		✔ McDonald's or the pizza parlor will do for a while		
Grocery Shopping When the Larder Is Bare	✔			
Washing Dishes		✔ if you use paper plates		
Washing Pots and Pans	✔			
Vacuuming		✔ until dust starts to obscure your vision		
Washing the Floors		✔ unless you spill the honey		
Cleaning up the Accident the Dog Had in the Corner	✔			
Learning to Use the Washing Machine or Assigning Someone Else to the Task	✔			
Ironing		✔		

ESSENTIALS AND NONESSENTIALS

	MUST BE GIVEN PRIORITY	CAN BE POSTPONED	SHOULD BE POSTPONED	SHOULD BE AVOIDED AT ALL COSTS
Polishing the Furniture		✔		
Taking Out the Garbage	✔			
Shoveling Snow from the Front Steps, Walk, and Driveway or Assigning Someone Else to the Task	✔			
Mowing the Lawn		✔		
Weeding the Garden		✔		
Taking All Safety Precautions, Including the Care of Your Car	✔			
Learning to Balance Your Checkbook	✔			
Attempting to Understand Your Financial Situation	✔			
Investing the Life Insurance Money in Get-Rich-Quick Schemes				✔
Taking Whatever Steps Are Necessary so Your Dependents May Go on with Their Lives	✔			
Coping with the Grief of Your Children	✔			
Coping with the Grief of Friends and Relatives		✔		
Fulfilling Job Responsibilities	✔			

ESSENTIALS AND NONESSENTIALS

	Must Be Given Priority	Can Be Postponed	Should Be Postponed	Should Be Avoided at All Costs
Deciding to Start a New Career			✔	
Putting One Foot in Front of the Other	✔			
Dulling the Pain by Drinking Yourself into a Stupor				✔ same goes for drugs
Deciding to Take the Pills You've Saved and End It All				✔
Deciding to Live with Your Mother/ Father/ Son/ Daughter			✔	
Deciding to Move			✔	
Deciding Whether or Not You'll Ever Marry Again			✔	
Trying to Find Answers to the Questions: How and when will I be okay? Why should I put one foot in front of the other?			✔	
Responding to These Questions: How much did he/she leave you, dear? Can I just drop by? (when asked by people of the opposite sex you didn't know very well)				✔
Watching for the Signs That Express Your Desire to Go on Living	✔			

their mysteries will be the main focus of our next chapter. Because one partner often takes charge of the financial affairs of the family, money matters are apt to loom, monsterlike, in the mind of the other, who may never have balanced a checkbook.

Certain household chores, like grocery shopping and feeding the dog, are also necessary to survival (your own, and certainly the dog's). Many find themselves in for a few nasty surprises when faced with these tasks for the first time.

When Ben's wife died, he immediately secured permission to take a leave of several weeks from his job. He wanted to make sure he would be at home and accessible when his sons needed him. He vacuumed, cooked dinners, and spent evenings talking with his boys. Just when he thought he was getting things under control, he ran out of socks. "Where are my clean socks?" he yelled down the hall. "I don't have any underpants," Denny called back. When it dawned on them that nobody had done the wash, their precarious world unraveled again.

Women are not immune to household problems either.

In the late fall, some months after Joe's death, Susan sat with her three eldest daughters in the living room of the new addition watching the first snowfall of the season. The twins had taken their sleds out, and the sight of their exuberance as they sped down the hill on their stomachs was heartwarming. As night fell and the scene faded, the family sat around the dinner table sipping hot chocolate until bedtime.

The next morning, when the older girls prepared to leave for school, they were surprised to find that the front door wouldn't open. "Hey, Mom! The door is stuck!" they shouted. Mom gave the door a healthy shove. It didn't budge. She looked out the window. The snow, she saw, had turned to sleet during the night, and the bank against the door was frozen solid. Nobody had thought to shovel. The girls went to school via the backdoor until the ice melted a week later.

However, the tasks were divided in your marriage, you will now have to deal with all of them by yourself, or develop strategies of trustworthy delegation. Don't hesitate to accept help (with chores, phone calls, meals) when it is offered, and try to ask for what you need. Often, doing something will help the helper as much as it will you. Your next-door neighbor may not realize that you don't know how to operate the washing machine, and your brother may feel better shoveling than pacing the floor wondering what he can do for you. When looking for help, remember that the people you need around you are your closest friends and relatives.

Besides financial matters and household tasks, crucial health and safety measures must also be put into place. We have given these important issues a chapter of their own (Chapter 3).

During this early stage of grief, you must concern yourself with what is necessary *and nothing else*! Defer all unnecessary decisions, minor and certainly major. Your ability to make them will come, but right now you have many more significant things to do.

Although life may appear more complex to those of you who live with dependents, the needs of dependents, even if sometimes frustrating, will often provide you with a respite from the pain of your bereavement, as you are forced—temporarily at least—to concern yourself with the care and comfort of someone else. (Sally, who was saving up the tranquilizers, was spared suicide by the needs of an ill sister who depended on her.) Children too have physical and emotional needs that must be met, and you have to find within yourself the strength to see that life goes on for them.

The process of restoring minimal order—and thus taking the first step toward rejoining the human race—is easier for some than for others. Dependents, a compelling job, or a meaningful hobby are forces that will hasten your return to life's mainstream. Those without dependents, who were forced to give up all outside interests while caring and fighting for a terribly sick spouse, have less tangible connections to life's pull. If you are one of these, your willingness to allow friends and loved ones (or a support group) to enter your world can hasten your progress.

Some friends will be better supporters than others

because of their own experiences, their personalities, or their commitment to you.

Carolyn came east from New Mexico when Margaret's husband was killed in an automobile accident. She decided to stay with her friend until Margaret could safely function on her own. Carolyn listened sensitively and then set up some objectives that she felt needed to be met before she could leave. She began by creating situations in which Margaret could practice regaining control. Starting at the most primary level (Margaret could not swallow and had eaten nothing for days), Carolyn ingeniously served slippery avocados on top of everything. She then steered Margaret through her fearful avoidance of driving, leaving the house, shopping for groceries, and paying bills, until Margaret was once again—at least minimally— upright and walking. Carolyn's absolute conviction that Margaret would be "okay" was tremendously strengthening, even though it was never verbalized. Carolyn knew that Margaret would not crumble, even though Margaret did not know this.

For younger widows and widowers, help is often complicated by the fact that neither they nor their friends have ever experienced a significant death.

Not long after Joe died, Susan learned of the death of her friend Elizabeth's husband. Elizabeth too was now a young widow, thrust into the position of caring for and coping with three teenagers by herself. Although Elizabeth lived almost two hundred miles away, Susan called her. The conversation that ensued was so mutually supportive and enlightening that the two women quickly ordered a service from their respective telephone companies that enabled them to talk before eight o'clock in the morning at a reduced rate. From then on (and for many years to come), they spoke weekly over a morning cup of coffee, sorting out their problems and their days.

Even with close friends at hand willing to help, those who have always been family nurturers may find themselves especially disconcerted and uncomfortable with the idea of suddenly being comforted.

"I am acting in a way I have never acted before," Barbara said. "I am taking instead of giving." Barriers broke down when she was able to admit, "I have gone through something traumatic."

What she had gone through was the experience of nursing her dying husband at home until his death while caring for four small children. By letting down the boundaries of her former role, Barbara was able to take the first step toward recovery.

Measure your progress during this immediate bereavement period by learning to recognize the signs that say, "I am alive." A helper may spot them sooner than you do. Although some may appear insignificant, do not minimize these accomplishments!

Eating, bathing, and dressing are actions that acknowledge that you are alive even if your spouse is not. And, although you may not be in touch with it, there is a part of you that wants to live. You will see it when you find yourself smiling at something, choosing to wear one sweater instead of another, planting a flower, petting an animal. Count these things up; they are the beginning of healing. They are the voices of your innermost being telling you that, tough as it may be, you are going to choose to live.

The chart on pages 15–17 may help you determine some of the priorities we've mentioned in this chapter.

POINTS TO REMEMBER

1. Recognize the signs of shock, understanding that the feelings they mask will emerge when they are ready.
2. Accept these painful feelings when they do emerge, and give them the space they need to run their course.
3. Do whatever is necessary (without harming yourself or others) to make it through another day and night.
4. Express your feelings to trusted friends and family, a support group, or a competent professional.
5. Remember that the people you need around you now are your closest friends and relatives.
6. Understand that the responses to grief are many and varied, and do not judge your own reactions by anyone else's standards.
7. Tackle only those tasks that are absolutely necessary, and postpone all others.

8. Make no major decisions.
9. Try to master the complexities of your financial situation.
10. Confine your losses by taking care of your own (and your family's) health and safety.
11. Attend to the household chores that are necessary to survival.
12. Accept offers of help.
13. Ask for help when you need it.
14. Do whatever is necessary to meet the physical and emotional needs of your dependents.
15. Maintain your job responsibilities.
16. Keep up your former interests, even though they may for a time appear meaningless.
17. Allow friends and family to enter your life.
18. Distinguish the individuals who are good supporters from those who are not.
19. Accept comfort and support even if it feels awkward at first to do so.
20. Learn to recognize the signs that say, "I am alive."

2 | For Richer or Poorer

I've got sixpence,
Jolly, jolly sixpence.
I've got sixpence
To last me all my life
—OLD SONG

*C*arrie took pride in paying her bills
promptly. With the nest egg of a sizable payment from Peter's life
insurance policy and the monthly addition of Social Security benefits
safely tucked into her checking account, Carrie felt flush—almost
wealthy. Each month she was surprised by the feelings of efficiency
and virtue that swept over her as she made her way through the stack
of bills, signing each check with a flourish. Details, like a running
record of her bank balance, didn't concern her, and bank statements

were tossed unopened into a bottom drawer. After all, what really mattered was that she didn't owe anybody a cent.

Then one day, on the crest of an uneasy whim, Carrie decided to open her bank statement. She was appalled when she discovered that there was barely enough money left to cover her living expenses for the next month. The insurance payment had evaporated, and Social Security benefits didn't come close to meeting her and her small son's financial needs. Carrie was forced to put their home on the market. She began searching desperately for a job.

Unconsciously, Carrie had denied the financial consequences of Peter's death, continuing to spend just as she had when Peter's paycheck had regularly been added to their account. Carrie's unwillingness to understand and accept her financial situation precipitated a traumatic move (which might have been avoided) and deprived her of the choices that a realistic assessment of her present and future needs would have allowed. The delayed and fateful opening of a bank statement forced Carrie, once again, into a victim's role.

People tend to have peculiar attitudes about money, and unfortunately times of trauma seem to heighten this tendency. At the top of the seesaw perch the gamblers (Carrie took a devil-may-care, let-the-chips-fall-where-they-may approach); at the bottom the penny-pinchers hold fast.

Even in the best of times, Richard was careful about money. His checkbook was meticulous; his records were always up to date. When his wife, Robin, decided to take a job, Richard applauded her decision, and as Robin's rainy-day dollars piled up in their savings account, Richard daydreamed about the backyard swimming pool they would soon be able to afford.

When a sudden heart attack took Robin's life, Richard's anger over his loss began to govern both his life and his finances. Although Richard's salary alone provided his family with both needs and comforts, he panicked. First, he stopped the milk and newspaper deliveries; then he took a second job. Each evening after work, he supervised the family's dinner. Then, changing from office clothes into more casual attire, he left his children with a baby-sitter and set off to drive a taxi until the wee hours of morning.

The anger that Robin's death provoked blinded Richard to the reality of his stable financial condition, and to the emotional needs of his children as well. Without Robin's love and support, Richard felt there was nothing left in life but monetary responsibility, and he was going to be responsible if it killed him.

It almost did. A doctor's diagnosis of a serious ulcer finally forced Richard out of his cab and into a more realistic understanding of his financial situation.

Most of us, during life's calm and content stretches, incline toward either the gambler or the penny-pincher personality. However, a tragedy can turn these latent tendencies into operating traits. If you are suddenly spending all of your savings dollars on lotto or are starting to stash cash beneath your mattress, it's time to take a long and careful look at the monies you have and the emotional attitudes that govern their use.

It seems unfair that a time of such stress, exhaustion, and helpless bewilderment should necessitate the immediate, shrewd, and knowledgeable handling of financial matters, but that is exactly what is required of you now. At the point when it is most difficult, you must walk out into the world and attempt to make intelligent decisions about the assets that have been left in your care.

You will have difficulty concentrating. You will probably wish you were home in bed. Often, you may be close to tears. *Nevertheless, the attempt to understand your financial situation must be made at once!* The leaves can lie unraked and cobwebs can drape gracefully from your ceilings, but matters pertaining to financial security must be met head-on and immediately. If you do not take control of them in the beginning, when choices still exist, they will eventually take control of you, leaving you no choices at all. So, before you pass out the paper plates and run down to Sal's for another pizza special with no anchovies, call your lawyer and make an appointment to see him or her as soon as possible.

Your lawyer will take charge of all matters pertaining to your spouse's will. If you can, see the lawyer who drew up the will and who has handled your family's legal and financial affairs up to this point. If you have no lawyer, get the best recommendations you can from the people you trust most.

There is a charge for handling a will. Some lawyers base their fee on the estate, charging 4 or 5 percent of what has been left to you. Other lawyers simply charge their standard hourly fee, which varies in different parts of the country. Ask your lawyer about the fee before you ask anything else, and be wary of lawyers who can't give you a pretty fair idea of what their work will cost you.

Your lawyer is the person who will be able to tell you what has been left to you. You will not, however, receive your inheritance immediately. First, the will must be probated (proved legal). If your spouse died without a will (intestate), the wait will be longer. (Laws governing the inheritance of an intestate death also differ from state to state, so if you live in California, don't check your facts with a friend in Wyoming.)

After you have contacted your lawyer, start investigating the life insurance benefits you may be owed. These don't just magically appear in your mailbox; you have to file a claim for them. To determine the kind of policy your spouse had (if you don't already know), go through all the insurance papers you can find in the desk—or in any other place where important papers may be hidden in your home. Death claims are sometimes appended to the backs of health, mortgage, business, or automobile insurance forms, so look carefully through everything that pertains to insurance. If you can't find anything but you know your spouse had life insurance, look through his or her old checkbook stubs for records of premium payments; there you should find the name of the company that holds the policy. Without the company's name, there is nothing you can do until the next premium comes due and the bill arrives.

If all you can find is the name of the company, call them. They will know the kind of policy your spouse had, and they will tell you what benefits you can expect from it. (Your spouse decided, when he or she bought the insurance, who its beneficiaries would be.) The insurance company will ask you for proof of your identification (your birth certificate, marriage certificate, or driver's license) and for proof of the death of your spouse.

The piece of paper which proves that you are not just making up a story is called a death certificate. When you are born, your parents get your birth certificate, and when your spouse dies, you get his or her death certificate. You must obtain it from the town clerk. It's a good idea to get a dozen or so copies on the first trip, because many agencies and companies require this proof, and subsequent trips for more death certificates are disheartening. A good funeral director will offer to obtain them for you. If the offer is made, accept it. If not, request it, and spare yourself the miserable task.

Your insurance company will need a copy of the death certificate, and they will ask you to file a claim form. Fill it out and send it to them. When your claim has been processed, you will receive their check. You may not get it immediately, but you'll want to file for it as soon as you can because you can't put your benefits to good use until you get them.

If your spouse's death was in any way work related, the possibility of workers' compensation should be investigated next. Here, again, your lawyer is the person to guide you through the legalities that apply to your particular situation. These legalities too can be time consuming.

It may come as a shock to learn that, for perhaps a couple of months after the death of your spouse, you have no money at all. Borrow from a friend or relative if you have to, and don't feel ashamed if you are needy; you are not the first person—nor will you be the last—to get caught short at a time like this. The probating of wills, insurance payments, Social Security benefits, and job-related benefits are all wound up in large amounts of red tape that take time to unravel. The next red tape to be tackled is that of Social Security.

Look up "United States Government, Health and Human Services Department, Social Security Administration" in your phone book, and then go to the office nearest you. Take your birth certificate, marriage certificate, divorce papers from any former marriages, and a copy of the death certificate. Take a good friend with you too; Social Security procedures can be intimidating, and it's good to have support. You will be asked to fill out forms (the first, unfortunately, of many), and you will be asked a lot of questions. Some of them may surprise you.

When Susan went to the Social Security office just two days after the memorial service for her husband, a man behind the desk shuffled through his papers, glanced frostily at Susan, and asked, "Was your husband a bigamist?"

"If he was," Susan replied timidly, "don't you think I'd probably be the last to know?"

When she later asked the icy man why he had posed such a question, he thawed a bit and wearily explained that, if her husband had been a bigamist, New York State would have been compelled to issue benefits to both wives and their respective families.

The benefits you eventually receive from Social Security will be based on the amount your spouse paid into the Social Security fund, your salary, and the number of minor children in your household. Once the checks start coming, they will arrive in the mail on about the same day every month, usually the third. If you prefer, you can arrange to have your checks deposited directly into your checking or savings account.

Social Security will, after this initial visit, contact you periodically (usually by mail) and will send you new forms to fill out, enabling them to stay abreast of your situation. There are, however, certain changes in your status or situation that you should report to them by phone, mail, or in person:

1. If you change your mailing address
2. If you earn more than the annual limit (they will inform you of what you are allowed to earn if you ask them)
3. If you go outside the United States
4. If you work outside the United States
5. If you are imprisoned for a felony
6. If you receive a government pension
7. If you remarry

8. If you adopt a child
9. If your children leave your care
10. If a child, nearing age eighteen, is disabled or is a full-time student
11. If a child eighteen to nineteen years of age who is a high school student drops out of school or graduates
12. If you become eligible for and receive a pension from work not covered by Social Security
13. If you are unable to manage funds
14. If someone in your household who is receiving benefits dies

Failure to notify Social Security of these changes may result in an overpayment to you. If you are overpaid, Social Security will take action to recover any payments not due you. To be forewarned is to be forearmed.

When Tom died, Elizabeth secured her license as a real estate broker and slowly began to save what she could toward college educations for her three teenagers. Social Security regulations then allowed recipients to earn an income of $6,000 above and beyond their benefits without forfeiting them. For a couple of years, Elizabeth earned more than the allowable $6,000. This, however, did not affect her monthly checks because of the exception to this regulation that allows a recipient to exceed the earnings limit if there are more than two minor children at home.

Ignorant of Social Security's regulations, Elizabeth rejoiced when she finally managed to send her first child off to college. Then, with only two children at home, she continued to exceed the earnings limit. Nothing happened. The checks continued to arrive in full, right on schedule. Then Social Security caught up with Elizabeth's income tax return and, realizing that she had been overpaid, stopped her benefits entirely.

Had Elizabeth reported her additional income, her own benefits would have been canceled, but she would have continued to receive the benefits owed to her two minor children. Elizabeth's failure to report her earnings resulted in the loss of all three benefits, because she now owed Social Security the monies that had been overpaid to *her. Almost $600 a month, on which Elizabeth depended, was cut off because she either was not informed of this regulation or did not understand it when she was informed. As the real estate market could best be described as lethargic during this period, Elizabeth had to work many long, long days to try to make up the difference.*

Stay informed of Social Security's regulations (which sometimes change from year to year), and don't be afraid to call their office if you have any doubts regarding their rules or your status with them. Dare to ask questions until you get the facts straight. Helping you is their job.

If a person should ever arrive on your doorstep saying he (or she) is from Social Security, ask to see identification before you speak with him or her. Warning bells should clang loudly if a "Social Security employee" ever asks you for payment for services rendered; the services of Social Security are free. If you have any doubt regarding a caller who says he or she is from Social Security, call their office and ask if they sent someone to see you. You don't need more troubles than you already have.

When you have met with your lawyer, filed your insurance claim, investigated work-related benefits, and notified Social Security of your status as a widow or widower, it's time to sit down and figure out what you will have in cash and assets and where it is located. Here again, it is wise to seek the advice of the lawyer or accountant who has been handling your family's financial affairs. Call and make an appointment for this purpose, and, while you await the meeting, search the house for bank statements, life insurance policies, deeds to properties, recent income tax returns, and your spouse's old checkbooks. Clear your musty drawers of anything that looks financial, important, or hopelessly confusing. Take all these records to your financial adviser, and take along a list of any questions you may have regarding your new economic situation. The records you find will enable you and your adviser to make a net worth calculation of monies and assets available to you.

With or without professional advice, you may want to use the following form as a guide to the type of information you will need to know. The figures called for here will help you gain a realistic assessment of your present financial situation. Fill in what you can on your own, and ask your financial adviser to help you in tracking down the evasive numbers.

NET WORTH CALCULATION

ASSETS

Liquid Assets

Cash and checking account(s)	$_____	
Savings account(s)	_____	
Life insurance cash values	_____	
Brokerage accounts	_____	
U.S. Savings Bonds	_____	
Other	_____	
Total Liquid Assets		$_____

Marketable Investments

Common stocks	$_____	
Preferred stocks	_____	
Bonds (corporate, municipal)	_____	
Other	_____	
Total Marketable Investments		$_____

"Nonmarketable" Investments

Tax–shelter investments	$_____	
Business interests	_____	
Vested profit–sharing/pension	_____	
Investment real estate	_____	
Notes receivable	_____	
Total "Nonmarketable" Investments		$_____

Personal Assets

Residence	$_____
Vacation home	_____
Personal property	_____
(autos, furs, jewelry, etc.)	

NET WORTH CALCULATION

ASSETS *(continued)*

Personal Assets

      Total Personal Assets $_____

      Total Assets $_____

LIABILITIES

Mortgages

    Residence $_____

    Vacation home   _____

    Investment real estate   _____

      Total Mortgages $_____

Loans

    Bank $_____

    Margin   _____

    Insurance   _____

    Other   _____

      Total Loans $_____

    Outstanding tax bills $_____

    Charge account, credit card balances $_____

      Total Liabilities $_____

      NET WORTH (assets minus $_____
             liabilities)

When you have figured out your net worth, you next need to make a realistic estimate of what your living expenses will be. If your partner was the family bill payer, you should be able to find most of the information you need in his or her old check stubs. Go back a year, and make a list of all the payments you can find for heat, electricity, telephone, mortgage, insurance, et cetera. Jot down the amounts and the months in which they were paid. The following form lists the expenses you need to determine.

ANNUAL CASH FLOW ANALYSIS

INCOME

Salary	$_____
Bonus	_____
Dividends	_____
Interest	_____
Partnership income	_____
Pension	_____
Social Security	_____
Other _____	_____
Other _____	_____
Total Income	$_____

DISBURSEMENTS

Expenses

Food	$_____
Clothing	_____
Transportation★	_____
Home maintenance/improvement	_____
Lawn care/snow removal	_____
Heat	_____
Gas and electric	_____
Telephone	_____
Mortgage payments/rent	_____
Contributions	_____
Gifts	_____
Vacation/travel	_____
Entertainment	_____
Education	_____
Interest payments	_____
Medical (unreimbursed)	_____
Insurance premiums	
Auto	_____
Homeowners	_____
Liability	_____
Health	_____
Disability	_____
Life	_____

ANNUAL CASH FLOW ANALYSIS

DISBURSEMENTS *(continued)*

Expenses
 Personal _____
 Professional services _____
 Other _____ _____
 Other _____ _____
  Total Expenses $_____

Debt Amortization
 Bank debt $_____
 Installment debt _____
  Total Debt Amortization $_____

Taxes
 Federal income $_____
 State and city _____
 Social Security _____
 Real estate (if not included in
  mortgage payments) _____
  Total Taxes $_____

TOTAL DISBURSEMENTS $_____

NET CASH FLOW (income minus disbursements) $_____

*Include gas, tolls, auto repairs, maintenance, registration fees, taxis, and public transportation.

When coping with finances, don't let fancy words like *disbursements* and *amortization* discourage you. A disbursement is an expenditure or payment, and you amortize a debt when you extinguish it gradually by installment payments; in other words, you pay it back little by little. Those who work in the world of high finance need, like everybody else, to feel important; they know full well that the casual mention of a word like *disbursements* or *amortization* adds weight to their proclamations. If when meeting with a high-minded financier you find yourself losing the drift of the conversation, speak right up and say so. Don't let a little thing like the fear of looking stupid trouble you for a minute; everyone feels stupid the first time she or he tries to understand a new and complex problem. Besides, you have been through worse.

When you have completed this form, go back to the list you made from your spouse's check stubs. Make a second list of all the months of the year, starting with the current one, and leave lots of space between them. Then, referring to your first list, write each anticipated payment under the month in which it is due. Keep this paper where you can find it. It will save you from going on a spending spree in April when all your insurance payments are due in May.

By the time you have gotten to the end of these calculations, you should have a good idea of whether or not you will need to modify your standard of living, and of how urgent it will be to do so. By paying off a debt with some of the life insurance money (and thus avoiding interest charges) or by cutting back on luxuries, you may find that you can get by without making radical changes in your life-style.

If your spouse had no life insurance, or if your life-style was dependent on two incomes and your financial picture is so bleak that a job, a job change, or a raise can't save it, you'd better consider selling your home or looking for a less expensive apartment. Stay in the same area if you can. The adjustments required by a move to a new community are many, and you don't want to go beyond easy reach of the friends whose support is so necessary now. When looking for a home, remember that manageability should be near or at the top of your priority list. There is only one person to carry the work load that used to be shared, and for several months you will be slowed down and distracted by your emotions. If it was your partner who cared for the plants, the serene and tempting garden of the house your realtor showed you yesterday will soon look as chaotic as you feel.

On the brighter side, it is quite possible that when the tallies are taken you will find yourself at the other end of the financial spectrum, with more cash on hand than you ever dreamed possible. Be careful. It is easy to let a large lump sum, like a life insurance payment, go to your head. Take another long look at your list of living expenses. Add $1,000, $5,000, or $10,000 to that figure for emergencies. Two or three months' living expenses usually constitute a practical emergency fund. Take a look around you too. Is your car beginning to balk? Is your roof starting to toss off its shingles? If you find you have an emergency in the making, add what you can to your fund to cover it before it happens, but stay within the limits of what you can afford.

Now, subtract your living expenses for one year, as well as your emergency fund, from the total monies available. The amount you have left represents the money you can invest for the purpose of bringing in additional income, or for just plain profit. Carrie, of the unopened bank statement, was unwise when she placed all her funds in her checking account; not only was her money too accessible there but it wasn't earning the interest that might have enabled her to keep her home.

The safe investment of your money calls for the most professional advice you can secure. Let your financial adviser know exactly what your economic situation is so that he or she can best determine the type of investment that is right for you. Let your adviser know how often you need the interest on your investments paid to you. Some investments yield interest yearly, some yield quarterly payments, while others can be set up so that they yield a monthly check. Before you plunk your money on the table, ask about the commission fee, and check that amount with a second source.

When considering any investment, remember this sage advice of old: if it sounds too good to be true, it probably is. With this in mind, avoid any solicitation for investments that promise

1. Fantastic returns in little or no time
2. "Insider" deals for the lucky few who see/hear the offer
3. "Can't lose" deals in which the salesperson has personally invested
4. Special investment secrets known only to the seller
5. Fabulous returns available only to those who act immediately

Once you have made the necessary decisions regarding the investment of your monies, you may, if you haven't done so already, wish to establish your own credit rating. Sometimes this experience can be eye-opening.

Margaret had carefully put all her credit cards into her own name as soon as the law was passed that established credit for wives. She then tried, on her first outing alone to a large city, to use a major credit card in a nearly empty store. Bells went off, lights flashed, and phones began to ring. Before she knew it, she was on the phone with a vice president who had clearly been waiting for just such an emergency. In full hearing of an intent and listening sales staff, Margaret was forced to repeat into the receiver: "You mean I can no longer use this card with my name on it because my husband was killed in an accident?"

Margaret was reduced to tears by this experience, and it took her hours to recover. Apparently this credit card company had not quite accepted what was by then federal law. Despite a letter of apology and the offer of a new card, Margaret no longer uses this particular line of credit.

To establish good credit, first pay your bills. The next thing to do—strange as it may seem—is take out a loan. Nobody wants to lend you money unless you've already borrowed money and paid it back. If you want to play the game, you have to play by the rules; take out a small loan, and pay it back promptly. Your credit rating will go up. Once your credit rating has been established, remember that you have the right of appeal if it is ever impugned. Use this right, and keep your economic flexibility intact.

These are the matters that, with an expert, you should discuss and consider while you are waiting for your monetary ship to come in. By the time it arrives, however, you will probably have accumulated a goodly stack of bills. In spite of your eagerness to remove any tinge of debt from your life, pay the bills slowly and carefully.

By the time Joe's will had been probated, the life insurance monies had been claimed, and the Social Security benefits had arrived in her mailbox, Susan felt as if there was no one in the world to whom she did not owe money. The telephone and electric compa-

nies had both sent her disconnection notices, and a book club to which her husband had belonged was threatening to send her to jail.

When her money had at last been deposited in her account, Susan sat down to a very long afternoon of check writing. For four hours she sat at her desk and worked her way down from the largest bill to the smallest. By the time she got to the last one, her back ached and she was seeing double. The very last bill in the stack was from the boy who delivered the Sunday New York Times each week, and it was for $4.58. Once paid, it would leave Susan with $352.48 in her checking account. Bleary-eyed and anxious to be done with the task, Susan mixed up the two figures; she wrote $4.58 in her checkbook as her balance, and she sent the delivery boy a check for $352.48. Now his ship was about to come in.

Three days later, before she even had time to notice her mistake, she found an envelope in her mailbox from the paperboy. Inside was her errant check with a scribbled note: "Don't you think you've made a little mistake?"

Indeed she had. And you will probably make some too. But you won't make as many if you develop a system for handling your financial responsibilities. Set aside a special day each month for payment of your bills and reconciliation of your checkbook balance with your bank statement. Most monthly bills arrive by the tenth and allow thirty days for payment; you might, therefore, choose the third Saturday of each month as bill-paying day. As you work, file paid bills in one drawer or shoe box and bank statements in another. A third drawer or box might be used for the papers you will need for tax purposes, while a fourth may come in handy for the safe storage of investment records. If this system doesn't work for you, adjust it to fit your needs. What matters is that your bills get paid on time and your records get placed where you can find them when you need them. In spite of mistakes that may be made along the way, you will through this process learn to take control of your own financial security. This is no small accomplishment!

Now that your monies and assets have been corralled and are safely headed for the barn, it's time to turn your attention to the management of your homestead, be it a cottage or a castle. A household headed by one individual presents many more challenges than one operated cooperatively. The first step toward meeting these challenges is to determine a list of priorities based on immediate needs. In an adult household, these include cleaning, cooking, shopping, home repairs, transportation, time management, and pet and plant care. Which of these tasks are most important to you, and on which can you afford to cut some corners? If you love gleaming floors but hate to cook, spend your time on your hands and knees and polish away, but fill your freezer with some of the tasty frozen dinners that line the supermarket shelves. If your dog's greeting fills your day with warmth but you find you have a black thumb, give your plants to your green-fingered friends. Try to reduce life's tasks to their simplest level. One woman we know read *Walden* for inspiration.

If you are alone and elderly, you may need to add to your budget an expenditure for some outside help. Do you need someone to assist with yard work? Would a cleaning person now and then make home seem brighter? If you don't drive, call on friends for transportation needs; perhaps you can baby-sit in exchange for a trip to the supermarket each week. If you don't cook, flatter your neighbors by asking for their advice and recipes. Investigate the services for senior citizens provided by your community. Follow all avenues that will connect you with others, and try to avoid spending too many long days by yourself.

That dated adage "A man may work from sun to sun, but a woman's job is never done" certainly applies to the widowed one with children still living at home, no matter which sex inherits these responsibilities. In addition to the chores just listed, these survivors must shoulder the tasks of child care, the monitoring of school attendance, transportation to extracurricular activities, supervision during school vacations, supervision and care during bouts of flu and chicken pox, and quality time for those they now nurture alone. If you are taking on these jobs for the first time, don't expect to have them all under control in a week or two, and don't be afraid to share your questions and anxieties with those more experienced. Talk to homemakers; ask working mothers how they do it. Try to determine any new expenses that may be required for the care of your children during periods when you must be elsewhere, and add them to your budget. Take the time to make sure that the care you select for your children is both capable and kind.

The demands of a full-time job combined with the never-ending needs of children can often seem overwhelming. You can ease that sinking-ship feeling by finding ways to take the time and space you need for yourself.

With a house full of teenagers, some of them too young to drive, Margaret found that the few hours she needed for herself were often borrowed from the hours that she had previously given to her children, who were, during this difficult period, immobilized without her. Live-in hired help was not a desirable option.

Margaret began to search for a solution to her problem, and she discovered that some of the local private schools had intern programs for recent graduates, all of whom needed housing. Margaret decided to try a barter system; she offered room and board—which she had in abundance (some of her children were now in college)—to one young woman she selected each year. Margaret's resident teenagers joined her in the selection process. In exchange, these young women were asked to assume the responsibilities of an older sister: driving when possible, listening when available, and acting as a helpful and friendly role model. This help allowed Margaret to travel when her work demanded it, to take a vacation without the children when she needed it, and to go out for early weekday moments with friends. The arrangement increased her own flexibility and the rest of the family's too. By scheduling her time and planning ahead, Margaret was able with this system to ensure that both her children and herself would have quality time.

Few survivors end up running their households exactly as they were run when their partner lived; one adult has limits that are less than those of two. And, as your standards begin gradually to shift from "ours" to "mine," you may find—in spite of the guilt that can accompany any change from the "ours" method of functioning—that you no longer wish for things to remain exactly as they were. Needs change. If your spouse was a commuter who caught the 5:15 train home and you met him or her at the station at 6:49, then you probably didn't get around to dinner until 7:15 or 7:30. Today you may find that a 6:30 dinner hour feels more comfortable. It may take a while, though, to realize that compromises over household issues are no longer necessary.

During the years of Susan and Joe's marriage, the home decoration decisions were usually left to Joe's professional eye and art school background. When a painting was purchased, it was always Joe who decided on the perfect spot for it. Although Susan secretly thought that the large naked lady who stared down at everybody was too much for the living room, she so enjoyed the relish with which Joe admired the results of his handiwork that she kept her objections to herself.

One night several months after Joe's death, Susan sat down in the living room to watch TV. It had been a bad day, and she was tired and depressed. When she looked up and realized that the large naked lady was watching her every move, it was more than she could handle. Furious, she marched into the kitchen, pulled out her stepladder, and pried the nude down. She felt better. Then she noticed how empty the wall looked. So she removed her favorite Carl Larsson prints from the hall and grouped them in the bare space the lady had left.

That night Susan spent hours rearranging paintings all over the house, and when she was done she sat back and admired her handiwork with relish. It seemed to her that even the house was grateful for the new life it had assumed with her efforts. It no longer felt like a museum that housed nothing but memories of the past. It had become once more a growing, breathing home.

The choices, now, are yours.

POINTS TO REMEMBER

1. In spite of the fact that you have every legitimate excuse in the world for not coping with anything right now, steel yourself, and take immediate control of your financial situation.

2. Call your lawyer and put your spouse's will, or lack of one, into his or her hands.

3. Contact your life insurance company, and take all the steps that will enable you to receive any benefits that may be owed to you.

4. Investigate workers' compensation if applicable.

5. Go to the town clerk and get about a dozen copies of the death certificate.

6. Go to the nearest Social Security office and apply for their benefits.

7. Stay abreast of Social Security's regulations, and report to them promptly any changes in your status.

8. It may take a couple of months for you to receive both inheritance and benefits, so borrow what you need to get you through this period.

9. Meet with your financial adviser (your lawyer or accountant) to determine what you will have in cash and assets and where it is located.

10. Make a realistic assessment of your financial situation based on the net worth calculation form in this chapter.

11. Estimate your living expenses by filling out the annual cash flow analysis form in this chapter.

12. Don't be afraid to speak up and ask questions (of your lawyer, accountant, Social Security representative, or other adviser) if anything at all confuses you. Understanding exactly what you're doing in the beginning can spare you numerous future problems.

13. If a weak financial situation requires that you sell your home, try to find another within easy driving distance of your friends, and choose a house or apartment that will be easy to manage.

14. If you are in the pink financially, invest your money wisely (with the help of an expert), and avoid going into the red.

15. Make an effort to establish a good credit rating.

16. Develop a system for bill paying and record keeping.
17. Take charge of your household by determining a list of priorities and cutting corners where you can.
18. If you inherit new child-care responsibilities, turn to friends for advice, and recognize that these tasks are monumental in scope and will require practice and patience to do well. Make the job easier by finding the time and space you need for yourself.
19. Anticipate any living expenses your new life-style may require, and add these costs to your budget.
20. Separate your own standards from those of your spouse, and make the decisions that will enable you to live comfortably with yourself and your family.

3 | Confining Your Losses

Life is just one damned thing after another.
—ATTRIBUTED TO FRANK WARD O'MALLEY

"Little pig, little pig, let me in!"
"Not by the hair on my chinny, chin chin!"
"Then I'll huff and I'll puff and I'll blow your house down!"
—NURSERY STORY

Disasters seem to strike in clumps. The annals of misfortune bulge with the histories of compounded tragedies: the jinxed widow who was robbed of all she possessed while attending her husband's funeral; the unfortunate fellow who totaled his car just four weeks after the death of his wife.

While some may view calamities such as these as pure and simple bad luck (albeit in the extreme) or choose to label their victims as accident prone, there is often a far more logical explanation. Distraction, and the all-too-likely carelessness it provokes, is often the foothold on which tragedies are founded and compounded.

Victims of loss are in constant danger of becoming victims of distraction as well. Exhausted by crisis and numbed by shock, they wander dazed through each long day and consider a home-cooked meal on the table to be nothing short of a miracle. (And they are right; under the circumstances, it is quite a feat!) In the process of getting that meal together, they overlook the appointment with the vet for the dog's booster shots or postpone the phone call to the oil company about the funny noises the furnace has been making, thus leaving the door wide open for "one damned thing after another" to walk in.

These are the days of potential jeopardy, when preoccupation with loss weighs so heavily that even the most basic tasks of survival require an almost superhuman concentration. The purpose behind the task may seem veiled or appear meaningless: Who cares if I eat or not? Why should I bother with a dentist appointment if I'm never going to smile again anyway? The forest of life's aims threatens to disappear completely behind the discouraging scrutiny of a single tree. The limited vantage point this perspective provides can lead to frustration and worse. The appointment you so carefully set up with your lawyer will get you no place if your car breaks down en route to the office. Your list of household priorities will become nothing more than additional intentions for that already well-paved road to you know where if you allow your own health to fail before you take the mop out of the closet. Good health, in fact, is at the top of this chapter's priority list, for without it there is little that can be accomplished. But don't let that scare you.

Margaret was forty when her husband was killed. In the time it took for a policeman to say a simple sentence, she became bereft, terrified, and the sole parent of four dependent children. Inclined even at the best of times toward hypochondria, Margaret soon became convinced that she would probably not live out the year.

Two months after Marv's death, worry won the battle, and she went to the doctor for a complete physical. In response to Margaret's concerns about her health, the doctor (an older and wiser woman) said, "Look, you may feel that your heart is broken, but there is nothing physically wrong with it. You may feel that you would like to fall apart, but you are not going to get off the hook that easily. You are as healthy as a horse." Margaret sighed, went home, and took the mop out of the closet.

While there is no question that our bodies are influenced by our psychological states (we blush with embarrassment, grow sick to our stomachs with fear, and so on), there is very little concrete evidence that bereavement causes physical illness (although it may encourage the development of some psychosomatic symptoms). Stress, however, can lower the body's resistance to illness.

While most healthy individuals can continue to function for a period of time in spite of inadequate nutrition and a lack of sleep (common symptoms of immediate shock and grief), those who were not in good health before the loss occurred run the risk of incurring additional complications when faced with the stress and deprivation that bereavement induces. (A controlled diabetic, for example, can be irretrievably harmed by inattention to diet.) Thus, the sooner one is able to return to those good physical habits of nourishment, sleep, and exercise, the less likely it becomes that one's body will suffer irreversible damage. If you are, like Margaret was, worried, or if you are troubled by symptoms you don't understand, don't hesitate to see a doctor at once; he or she may turn out to be just the ally you need.

The loss of a mate creates stresses in every area of your life. It robs you of everything that was once secure and familiar, leaving you a stranger to your home and even to yourself. The first step toward the relief of these pressures is to recognize the stress you feel as real and potentially harmful. The second step is to investigate the traditional methods of stress reduction that may be of help to you: letting your feelings out by talking with family and friends, and if needed with clergy or health-care professionals; taking note of hot lines or crisis intervention centers that may be nearby. You might try relaxation exercises—meditation, imagery, or yoga—as well as the physical exercise available in a variety of sports.

Margaret, in the earliest days of her grief, learned that she needed a five-mile walk by herself each day. Her stroll became her sorting-out time, a time to be alone, think things over, and struggle for acceptance of her loss. Without this quiet time, her ability to function in other areas of her life soon suffered. It wasn't until later, further along in grief and many miles down the road, that Margaret realized the physical advantages walking afforded her.

Healthful aids, like walking, are a far better alternative for rest and relaxation than artificial medications, which have a Jekyll and Hyde potential of transforming the dream of induced relaxation or sleep into a nightmare of addiction. Few of us go through grief without being tempted to numb ourselves artificially: prescribed drugs, unprescribed drugs, alcohol, tobacco, you name it—all lure with the promise of respite from pain. (Support groups for survivors are often filled with smokers; anyone who has ever smoked at any time of life becomes doubly vulnerable to a cigarette's charms when bereft of everything else that mattered.)

The danger of these temptations may be further compounded by an ambivalence, which often appears at this time, toward self-destructiveness. A subtle and insidious "Who would care if I died anyway?" mentality may applaud the normal carelessness of this period, prodding and goading it into an angry stand or a defiant test of fate.

John ordered one more martini for the road as he told the man on the neighboring bar stool the whole story of Karen's battle with incurable cancer. The sadness that filled his voice as he described the discovery of his wife's illness turned to fury as he relived her death.

"Can I give you a lift home?" his listener asked, worried about John's physical and emotional condition.

"I'll drive home alone," John snapped, "just like I'll do every-thing else from now on." He lurched for the door and stumbled down the walk to his car.

"I'll drive home drunk if I want to," John muttered angrily, groping for his keys. "If I'm meant to live, I'll make it; if I die, maybe I'll see Karen again." The only vague thought that troubled him was that Karen, he was certain, had gone straight to Heaven; with his luck, John figured, Hell was a distinct possibility for him.

John lost control of his car on the downward curve of a hill and careened through a meadow's underbrush until his progress was abruptly halted by a ditch. A passing motorist notified the police, and within half an hour John had been fingerprinted and charged with driving while intoxicated.

The martinis had not been conducive to the consideration of a nonfatal crash: the arrest, fine, suspension of license, criminal record, and so on—all of which greatly increased the unbearableness of John's already miserable day-to-day existence. The accident thrust John into a cycle of diminishing self-esteem and shattered his fragile faith in his ability to survive this difficult period of change and growth. For months afterward, John grieved—for Karen and for his tenuous hold on self-respect, which had snapped in a meadow.

Fortunately, despite seductive thoughts of artificial relief, most of us learn that we have more success when we cope with our lives and our pain undrugged. Too many doctors prescribe tranquilizers and sleeping aids routinely to those attempting to begin the gargantuan effort of rebuilding a life. When you use sleeping pills without restraint, you'll soon need a morning wake-up pill, and the vicious cycle escalates. Drugs don't solve problems; they merely postpone them and ultimately increase them. There are undoubtedly medical exceptions—ongoing medication, for instance, or the brief usage of sleeping pills to correct a no-sleep cycle. More often, however, addictive behavior only reinforces a victim mentality; you enter grief as a victim of loss, and you become a victim of both loss and drugs. This is a mentality you need to leave behind as soon as you can. You can do so by accepting responsibility for your own well-being. And it will help if those around you also recognize and accept the stress of your days.

Virginia, a prominent and conscientious English teacher in a small town, went back to her classroom shortly after her husband's sudden death. For several weeks she surprised everyone with her continuing effectiveness. Then shock wore off, grief took over, and Virginia began to feel as if she were disintegrating. She shared her feelings—although it was extremely difficult to do so—with superiors and requested a month-long leave of absence in the middle of the school year. Her superiors acknowledged and accepted her acute anxiety, found a temporary replacement, and granted Virginia her leave.

By recognizing her needs and taking charge of her own health and sanity, Virginia was able to use her leave as a time to think out her life and face her fears. A month later, she returned to school and, reorganized and capable, won the increased admiration of both students and faculty. Virginia's sense of self-worth grew in the process too, for she knew that she had recognized the beginnings of a negative progression and, by taking command, had stopped it cold.

Although time spent alone can evoke terror in a survivor's soul because of the enveloping pain that grows with silence, such time for thinking is something all survivors need to come to terms with the radical changes in their lives and the fears those changes produce. As most of us know, fears directly confronted in daylight are less frightening than avoided fears, which grow stronger in the dark.

One of the biggest fears a survivor may have to face is that of living alone. You can confront your fears directly by taking the steps that will make your home as secure as possible. Simple procedures—like the replacement of your name by your house number on your mailbox, the substitution of an initial for your name in the phone book, and the installation of a garage-door opener—will increase your sense of safety and your responsibility for your welfare. Battle absent-mindedness by leaving an extra house key with a neighbor, and bolster your defenses by having your house or apartment security checked by the police department. Fire and safety alarms and barking dogs offer additional protection, and the dogs, when not yapping, may provide comfort as well. If you are going away for a few days, stop newspaper and mail deliveries, alert the neighbors, and leave your home with a lived-in look: lights on timers, lawns trimmed, and so on. Good locks, simple precautions, and common sense can prevent most property crimes.

Guard your safety within your home by taking extra care when performing dangerous tasks. Avoid climbing high ladders without a helper nearby. Unplug the iron as soon as the last of the laundry is pressed. Keep dark hallways and outside steps well lit by replacing burned out light bulbs promptly. In freezing temperatures, store emergency rock salt in your garage for those nights that can turn your driveway into a glacier.

Be ever watchful for little household problems with serious trouble potential: the toilet that keeps clogging, the fuse that blows continually, the odd odor that wafts off the septic tank whenever the wind is from the west. If you are not handy with problems such as these, start a list of recommended plumbers, electricians, and other such professionals, and keep it near your phone. Call an expert at the first sign of trouble. While having to replace a furnace may be a nasty shock, it is not nearly as nasty as having to replace a house.

If you are elderly or have a history of health problems, take extra precautions. A Medic Alert, worn like a necklace, will, by your pressing a button, notify a hospital and ambulance of a problem. An automatic-dial phone that has been programmed with the numbers of family, friends, and emergency services can facilitate your call for immediate help. The formation of a network of friends who regularly check up on each other's whereabouts and welfare is a good idea too.

Selma, an elderly widow, was new to an apartment complex in a strange city. Through a senior citizens' group, she found three other individuals who lived alone and nearby. Together they formed a telephone chain that provided each of them with a one-minute call every morning. This simple precaution cost them nothing but the phone call, which started each day with a cheerful word. It also provided a double check on health, an assured notification if a phone was inoperative, and numerous bonuses, such as errands exchanged or shared as needed and friendship. Relatives and other friends— provided with all three network numbers for use when any member of the group could not be reached—were thus spared hours of worry.

If you have become a lone adult in a household of children, your need for security measures will be more complex. Make sure that children who come home to an empty house understand rules, routines, and safety precautions. Inform them clearly of their responsibilities, and live up to yours. Let them know where you will be when, and call—even if it's after bedtime—if you are unable to get home when you said you would. Children become just as frightened as you do when people they love and need are not where they said they would be. Avoid future problems by taking time each day to listen to your children. Find out how school is going, who their friends are, which baby-sitters they like and which they detest. Check out baby-sitters and day-care centers carefully. Ask for references and use them.

When dealing with plumbers, electricians, baby-sitters, and other service providers, keep your emotions in check. A woman alone with every toilet in the house backed up is likely to view the rescuing plumber as no less than a knight in shining armor. A business deal that suddenly hangs on the unexpected thread of a dinner invitation and Mrs. Jones's ability to baby-sit for three more hours may lead a desperate man to perceive a beauty in kindly Mrs. Jones that had hitherto passed unnoticed. In vulnerable times, relief and gratitude can easily be mistaken for true and undying affection. Try to keep these fleeting fantasies in perspective; say thank you to the plumber, and drive Mrs. Jones home.

A year after Joe died, faulty wiring in Susan's kitchen wall led to a serious fire. (Susan knew her wiring was haphazard but had neglected to have it checked.) Although the flames were confined to the kitchen, the air in the adjoining living room became so hot that the water in it vaporized and rained into the open grand piano. The piano, then Susan's lifeline, was severely damaged and had to be moved to a shop for repair. Terrified of facing life without it, Susan dreaded the arrival of the piano movers; she was afraid she would cry, disgracing herself in front of strangers.

On the morning the movers were expected, Susan gave herself a big lecture. I will be businesslike and professional, she told herself. I won't cry. Anyway, it's not as if a person's dying; it's just a piano. But she felt as if it were a person.

The movers came. Susan watched as three big men took the legs off her piano and turned it on its side. They wrapped it in quilts and carefully slid it across the room to the front door. Then, just as Susan was silently congratulating herself on her calm deportment, the biggest mover, peering over the side of the piano, said kindly, "It's sort of like she's going off to the hospital for an operation, isn't it?" Tears leapt to Susan's eyes at the unexpected understanding in the mover's voice. If at that moment he had asked her to join him, she would surely have followed him anywhere.

Following somebody is a lot easier than getting around town on your own. If you are new to the role of family driver, you may find that the supposedly simple logistics of getting from one place to another present some physical challenges that you overlooked when you were just a passenger. If you are not used to frequent driving and the responsibilities of maintenance that every car requires, join the American Automobile Association or a similar organization. Then find a dependable shop or gas station equipped to handle maintenance and repairs. Ask to be put on a schedule of tune-ups that will keep your car in top-notch running order. Make sure that the crucial mechanisms—brakes, steering, and tires—have been thoroughly tested for safety, even if doing so makes you feel like a nuisance.

If you need to buy a new car for the first time in your life, read *Consumer Reports* for the latest evaluations of new car performance, safety, and value. Solicit advice from knowledgeable friends. Without help, the contemplation of this enormous and critical investment can paralyze your capacities for decision.

When Sherry's children became teenagers, she suddenly needed a second car. The choices overwhelmed her completely. Day after day she postponed a decision, and the adolescent clamor swelled as the need grew in urgency.

Finally, still unable to cope with the ramifications of which car to choose, Sherry went out and bought a model that was exactly the same make and color as the one she already owned. Today, if you visit Sherry, you can still see—sparkling side by side in her driveway—the maroon twins born of her indecision.

Although many of us do not have the wide-open choice that Sherry faced, the selection process can still present problems.

Marilyn's driveway curved a quarter of a mile up a steep hill, which was impassable in snowy winters without four-wheel drive. When her old car began to shudder and wheeze as winter approached, Marilyn realized that she could no longer postpone this major purchase. She knew she wanted to buy a car that could be switched into four-wheel drive from the driver's seat, to avoid the discomfort of lying on the sloping ice while trying to adjust the hubcaps. The only car that offered this option had a standard shift. Marilyn had never driven a standard shift.

But that didn't stop her. Marilyn simply took a friend along to her local dealer. She then magnanimously offered her friend Rachel the opportunity of being the first person to drive her new car home.

Marilyn's fears mounted when Rachel departed, leaving her with a bright new car she couldn't drive. She walked out to admire it every day, she named it Scarlet (it was red), but it wasn't until almost a week later, when the refrigerator was bare, that necessity thrust her into the driver's seat. In spite of a hair-raising leap into the middle of an intersection, she managed to get the groceries home and save her children from starvation.

If you are looking for a used car, shop with an expert, or at least someone in whom you have implicit trust.

When the old and feeble family automobile she'd inherited from her husband finally broke down in her driveway one morning, Elizabeth was desperate. Her livelihood, real estate, depended on a working car. Elizabeth had an appointment to show a house that afternoon, $1,500 in the bank, and an automobile dealer she knew and trusted. She gave him a call.

"What do you have that's safe and reliable for fifteen hundred dollars?" she asked.

"A blue Vega," her dealer replied.

"I'll take it," Elizabeth said.

Her purchase was successful. The Vega lasted until Elizabeth managed to save enough to look for a newer model. (A word of caution: This unique, sight-unseen method of car purchase only works if the dealer's reputation is both sterling and proven.)

Whether your car is brand new or tried and true, remember to keep the doors and windows locked when you're driving. A flashlight and first aid kit in the glove compartment may come in handy, as well as a bag or two of sand (for weight and traction) and a snow shovel in the trunk. Individuals who drive often at night or for long distances will feel safer with a CB radio.

When traveling to a new place for the first time, carefully plan your route in advance. Most survivors feel lost enough as it is; they don't need the additional fear and humiliation of becoming lost in the literal sense.

Margaret had gone to the airport many times as a passenger but had never driven there herself. One day shortly after Marv's death, she departed for the airport to pick up her son, Adam, who was returning from a visit to a relative. Instead of examining a map, she checked directions with a toll collector and ended up completely lost in the middle of the night in a neighborhood she had never seen before. In total panic (an extremely dangerous way to drive), Margaret soon became convinced that she would miss her son's flight and most probably never find her home again. Never had she felt more lonely, scared, and out of control.

Although Margaret didn't make it to the airport that night (she called Adam and told him to take public transportation), she did find her way home. She determined then and there to chart all future routes clearly on a map before taking even one step in the direction of her car.

Know where you are going and how you intend to get there. Leave lights on at home if you won't be back until late. Park as close to your destination as possible, in an area that is well lit and will remain so until your return. Be particularly alert and careful when using underground and enclosed parking garages. Avoid shortcuts, little-used staircases, and dark, isolated spots. Carry a minimum of cash, and make sure that your credit cards, identification, license, and insurance cards are listed elsewhere; this will make it easier to let go of your purse if doing so will get rid of an attacker.

If your car breaks down despite your mapped route, safety precautions, and tune-ups, steer it to the shoulder of the highway. Turn on the flashers, raise the hood, get inside your car, and lock the doors. If strangers stop to help you, ask them to alert the police or nearest service station. (There is a banner, which can be purchased, that says, "Call police," but a homemade sign will convey the message just as well.) Do not roll down your window, do not let strangers into your car, and do not get into someone else's car—these are risks you can't afford to take.

Despite the internal chaos that emergencies provoke, an *appearance* of alertness and confidence can, of itself, help you avoid a variety of victimizing experiences. Preparing for the possibility of an emergency can help. Even something as basic as the clothes you wear can contribute to confidence.

When Bridget became a widow, she owned a wardrobe of around-the-house jeans, teaching skirts and sweaters, and some out-to-dinner finery. Suddenly and unwillingly propelled into a series of appointments with lawyers and accountants, she was faced with the option of appearing unsophisticated (and possibly naïve) in her teaching clothes or overdressed (and, heaven forbid, gaudy) in her out-to-dinner specials.

Bridget's friend Gwen stepped in and saved several days by buying Bridget a "dress for success" outfit. Knowing that she was appropriately attired helped Bridget function at a time when anything that contributed to her feelings of inadequacy might have stopped her from functioning altogether.

When you have added that lucky dress or sports jacket to your wardrobe, make a mental evaluation of the professional relationships you have inherited. You will now need a new will, a designated guardian for your minor children, a new way of paying your taxes, new health, car, and life insurance.

Did you like the lawyer who handled your spouse's will? Was the fee fair and reasonable? Did your accountant give you clear and meaningful advice?

When her husband died suddenly, Lilly inherited an estate that required the services of a large accounting firm. At first, she attributed her difficulty understanding the advice of these professionals to shock. However as months passed the crucial issues these men handled became no clearer. The answers to her most basic questions seemed to strand her in a jungle of legal verbiage. When she attempted to hack her way through to comprehension, she ran into quicksand dismissals: "We already explained that to you" or "Just send the check." Tired of receiving condescension when what she needed was education, Lilly resolved her dilemma by firing the firm.

She packed up her business and took it off to a woman accountant she'd discovered who had the knowledge, patience, and ability to help Lilly understand and control her finances. Today Lilly often finds, to her amazement, that she does not "owe this amount" and that sometimes even the IRS makes mistakes.

Now, even though you are miserable, is the time to take charge of these crucial issues that can and will affect the quality and security of your future. And there *is* a future out there. Now is the time to take the steps that will keep the big, bad wolf from your door and minimize the possibility of "one damned thing after another" taking over your life and utterly convincing you that "everything always happens to me." These steps are the beginning of a reanchoring process that will soon make you responsible for your own and your family's well-being. These are the measures that, once taken, will slam the door on the destructiveness of a passive victim mentality.

Almost everyone knows what happened to the little pig who built his house of straw. Perhaps it was distraction that led him to choose straw as a building material simply because it was easily obtainable. (Who had the energy to look for bricks?) Besides, what did it matter if the big, bad wolf came? That sad little pig learned too late that it did matter. (For those of you who missed this story, the big, bad wolf blew the little pig's house right down.)

The smart little pig who built his house of bricks wasn't taking any chances. Don't you take chances either. By recognizing and learning to control grief's distraction and carelessness, you can actively contribute bricks to the solid foundation of your new life. By preparing in advance for the possibilities of emergency, you can dash the nighttime fears that banish sleep and diminish the anxiety that surrounds your days. If your driveway turns to ice or your car breaks down, you will be ready to cope with the problem. Or if the big, bad wolf should decide to come down your chimney, you will have the inner strength that comes from knowing where the kettle is. Your preparedness to cook him will give you peace of mind.

POINTS TO REMEMBER

1. Absorption in grief makes you distracted, and this is dangerous.
2. Safeguard your health by returning to good habits of nourishment, sleep, and exercise as soon as possible.
3. Recognize and accept the stress your loss has induced, and seek the means of stress reduction that work best for you.
4. Keep reminding yourself that drugs don't solve problems. Often they increase them.
5. Beware of a tendency toward self-destructiveness that can make you careless.
6. Avoid becoming the prisoner of victim mentality by taking responsibility for your own well-being.
7. Realize that time alone to think—even though it is scary—will help you face and accept the radical changes in your life.
8. Take any steps that may be needed to make your home as secure as possible.

9. Be especially careful when performing any dangerous tasks in and around your home.

10. Keep your eyes and ears open for little household problems with serious trouble potential.

11. Keep your emotions in check when dealing with those who provide emergency services; marry the plumber if you will because you love him for himself, not because he unclogged your john.

12. If you are elderly or in poor health, provide yourself with access to help in an emergency.

13. If you have children at home, make sure they are informed of all household rules and safety precautions.

14. Put your car on a schedule of regular maintenance and tune-ups.

15. When driving, know where you are going and how you intend to get there.

16. Carry a minimum of cash when traveling.

17. Learn to recognize possible emergencies and prepare for them before they occur.

18. Dress in a manner appropriate to the situation, in clothes that enhance your self-confidence, particularly when dealing with lawyers, accountants, and other such professionals.

19. Evaluate the professional relationships you have inherited, and discard those that don't help you.

20. Start your new life safely by learning to recognize and control the distraction and carelessness that grief provokes.

Part II

GRIEF WORK

4 | Grief: The Valley of the Shadow

Give sorrow words; the grief that does not speak
Whispers the o'er-fraught heart, and bids it break.
—WILLIAM SHAKESPEARE, MACBETH

*W*hen Susan was a child, she loved to read books about brave and tragic heroines. She marveled at Jane Eyre, who with amazing moral courage turned her back on great love (leaving poor Mr. Rochester to cope with his deranged wife) and resolutely walked into the wide, wide world alone. Little Women was an inspiration too. Susan wept as sweet Beth slowly died, transcending fear and pain through consideration of those around her as she faded into oblivion uttering kind words to all.

Susan would spend hours picturing herself as a tragic heroine. She would, she imagined, be pale and thin—but beautiful nonethe-

less—and she would sit beneath a willow tree, concealing her own pure and simple sorrow (over something vague and unspecific) with a sad smile as she knit exquisitely executed socks for soldiers going off to war. In fact, Susan spent many hours of her childhood eagerly longing for tragedy to strike.

Years later, when tragedy did strike, Susan felt somehow cheated by the realization that the image she was projecting was nothing like the vision of those childhood daydreams. In real life Susan gained weight, developed an increasingly unkempt appearance, and dulled her sorrow in Scotch. The proverbial willow tree was under attack from gypsy moth caterpillars; if she had sat under it, she would have been covered with little green worms.

There is nothing romantic about coping with the death of one's partner for life. The catchall word describing the attempt to do so is *grief.* The first definition the dictionary offers for this word is "Intense mental anguish; deep remorse, acute sorrow or the like." If grief amounted to nothing more than pure and simple sorrow, one could weep and be done with it. But the intense mental anguish provoked by a loss of this magnitude has an emotional content far more confusing than straightforward sorrow. And while suffering is ultimately supposed to breed character, and grief to ennoble, it is the *lack* of character and nobility that one initially notices.

This is because the many emotions that constitute the expression of grief are highly complex and often contradictory. They include love and jealousy, anger and guilt, loneliness and self-pity, deprivation and sadness, fear and helplessness, bitterness and emptiness, self-hatred, apathy, and numbness. These feelings usher in the emotional freeze that covers solid ground with ice, making movement in any direction seem precarious and dangerous. Growth is hidden, progress seems blocked, and one bleakly speculates that just because the crocuses made it through the snow last year is no reason to believe they can do it again this year. It's not a pretty picture.

Although sorrow may have made its entrance during an illness that led to death, grief moves to center stage sometime after the funeral, when the adrenaline (which flowed so copiously during the time of emergency) disappears and when shock ceases to dull the edges of pain. The period of grieving, which can last anywhere from several months to a few years, encompasses the length of time required to say good-bye to a love and a life-style, and to gather the strength and courage needed to begin anew and alone.

These are the days that seem to hang, forever suspended, between a lost past and an unfathomable future. And, as the minutes tick slowly and relentlessly toward the unfathomable, the attention of friends (who stood by you during the funeral and the days shortly thereafter) lessens. Your mother (father, daughter, son) goes home. The meals, delivered by neighbors when the emergency was at its peak, disappear. And after the initial round of goodwill dinner invitations, the calendar, like the rest of your life, may become nothing more than a collection of the empty squares of unplanned days. As those who dropped everything to comfort you begin to step back into the events of their more normal days, you start to feel isolated. Alone, with insomnia for a bedfellow and exhaustion for a daily companion, you struggle to find a meaning in your loss and a purpose for your days.

The struggle for understanding and acceptance of loss is complicated by the fact that the experience of grieving varies greatly from individual to individual. For a long time psychologists and theoreticians attempted to define normal responses to acute grief and suggested that variation from the patterns they outlined was a sign of pathology. We are fortunate to live in a time when those ideas are being challenged. There are, however, several characteristics that most bereavements hold in common.

Elisabeth Kübler-Ross, observing people who were aware of their terminal illnesses, noted the following stages: denial and isolation, anger, bargaining, depression, and acceptance. She suggested that bereaved individuals go through similar stages. Awareness of these stages can be a valuable tool for survivors who are desperate to find order in the chaos of overwhelming emotions in which they are ensnared. But it is important to remember that this is only an organizational tool—a way to name things. Not everyone experiences every one of these stages, no one experiences them in a linear progression, and, of course, the stages look far tidier on paper than they feel in real life. Some individuals may travel through all or most of these stages in the space of an afternoon, only to awaken the next morning and begin all over again. (Do not underestimate how hard this is!) Others may find themselves blocked by just one aspect of the process. Some survivors seem to spend most of their days wading through the murky waters of depression, while others may bog down in the muddy swamps of anger or denial. Alice, five years after the death of her husband, said,

"Denial was one of the biggest feelings. I never went back to my beautician because I couldn't face telling her. And I wouldn't go to a place if my husband and I had gone there together. I was angry with him, too, for putting me in that position. . . . and guilty if I laughed. I needed someone to tell me it was okay to enjoy myself, but guilt was always in the back of my mind."

Those who experience a prolonged period of denial are (like those in shock) protecting themselves from absorbing the entire impact of their losses at any single moment. These mourners circle their losses, glancing at them quickly out of the corners of their eyes, choosing not to look at them at all during periods of raw vulnerability when the pain of realization is too great to handle. The eagerness for a speedy recovery wars with the self's protection of a personality not yet ready to bear the full extent of the pain that accompanies loss.

At one of the meetings of the support group for widows and widowers that Lilly headed, Catherine, who had recently lost her husband, confronted Lilly angrily:

"When will I feel better?" she asked. "Will I ever get over it?" Then, turning to Lilly in despair, she asked, "When did you get over it?"

"I've been a widow for eleven years," Lilly responded. "Can we assume that I have 'gotten over it' and accepted the reality?" Catherine nodded. "Let's assume," Lilly continued, "that I got up one morning and felt that I was 'over it.' My husband is dead. I am a

*widow. I must face life alone." She turned to the group before her.
"How do you think I felt that morning?" she asked.*

*The group was very quiet, and then they answered: "awful,"
"sad," "frightened"* . . . *and they understood why one does not want
to accept, and in fact cannot accept, the full extent of one's loss for a
while—at least not until one is strong enough to know that one can
survive.*

The chart on the next page developed by Dr. Roberta
Temes plots the stages and characteristics of the grieving process in the framework of the time it may take to move from
one stage to the next until gradual acceptance is reached.
(Once again, we caution that these stages and the times allot-
ted for them can vary greatly from individual to individual.)

While time, as we can see, distances, it does not by itself
heal. It can, however, be used constructively to promote
healing. Judy explains it this way:

*"I think I understood my husband's death intellectually, but it
took a long time and a lot of introspection to accept it fully. I wanted
him back. I went up and down. I'd go so far down I'd think I could
never get back up. It takes lots of times of being back down in that
hole to realize that you've been there before, and to know that
you'll come back. At some point, you begin to see the pattern and to
accept it."*

One may quickly understand intellectually, the stages
and emotions that constitute grief, but it takes far longer to
experience those stages and emotions internally. This, however, is what grief demands. There is no intellectual shortcut
through its maze.

*Nine months after his wife's long and painful death, Bob felt
that he had a handle on things. While he had plunged back to work
with a vengeance (in fact, he had been promoted), he had also taken
the time to examine the feelings and emotions of grief about which he
had read. He could now look back on those months of loss and doc-
ument the moments of isolation, denial, anger, and depression—the
very stages through which he had helped his wife. With the support
of a widowed people's group, he had begun to expand his social
network (only to people who had lost spouses) and had even attended
two parties. At one of these parties, he met and made friends with a*

STAGES	DURATION	CHARACTERISTICS	NEEDS	TASKS	HELPER FUNCTIONS
Numbness	Several weeks or months	Mechanical functioning Insulation	Need for privacy, to be with one's pain; nonetheless, need for caring friends	To protect self from feeling impact of loss	Assist in practical way, chores, etc.
Disorganization (yearning, transitional tasks, anger, guilt, ambivalence, acting crazy)	Many months	Painful feelings: loneliness depression weeping Sleep and appetite difficulties Sorrow for self Hallucinations	Intimacy, ventilation of feelings	Acknowledge impact of loss	Permit expression of *all* feelings Listen
Reorganization	Months	Occasional peacefulness Less intensity of feelings	Encouragement to enter life again	Resolve relationship with deceased	Expand social network

woman whom he eventually asked for a date. Unexpectedly, that date turned into his first sexual encounter since his wife's death.

The next morning, Bob found himself at the cemetery. He felt that he had regressed to square one; nearly a year had passed, but Bob found himself thinking of his wife as though she were alive.

Bob was furious with himself and terribly frustrated. At the next group meeting, he railed about being "stuck in the pits." The incident thrust him back into the grip of an incredible depression.

In a way, Bob's intellectual comprehension of the process had led him straight down one of grief's proverbial garden paths. What Bob had learned through this experience was that grief requires gut responses, not cerebral ones.

What then, on a gut level, does a day of grief feel like?

If you have slept, you find yourself awakening with an arm outstretched to touch the body no longer beside you in bed. When the shock of loss has washed over you for the hundredth time, anger at the outrageous desertion may be the next emotion to take hold.

Anger can encompass several feelings, such as fear, bitterness, guilt, and self-hatred. Anger toward someone you love is an uncomfortable emotion. Anger toward someone you love who is dead feels downright small and mean. It may give you the uneasy suspicion that you are adding the zenith of insults to the ultimate of injuries. Furthermore, anger toward one who is dead leads inevitably to frustration; it is like trying desperately to argue a point with someone who is giving you the silent treatment. Anger that is blocked may be directed elsewhere—at the bickering of married couples, for instance, or at a friend who calls to discuss a marital problem. When the expression of anger is blocked completely, you become depressed.

Dr. Willard Gaylin, a psychiatrist at Columbia, suggests, "If you feel you need the other person to cope with life, then they threaten your very survival by dying. You feel abandoned. Anger then triggers guilt. Guilt, in turn, leads to depression, which is a form of self-punishment for feeling angry."

Survivors who feel angry toward one they love and on

whom they depended don't feel very good about themselves. And as anger builds the feelings of panic and insecurity that accompany loss become compounded with guilt and self-hatred. Unfortunately, these new and painful feelings are often reinforced by outsiders. Anger is not an emotion that evokes sympathy and compassion in those to whom a survivor must now turn for emotional support and practical help. Although clinically it has long been recognized as a valid component of the grief process, socially anger remains threatening. The survivor is now on a collision course, caught between his or her real feelings and the need for acceptance. Unable to confide in those he needs for today's survival, and unable to live another moment in the isolated world in which anger, guilt, and self-hatred threaten to engulf the very love that has always been his mainstay, the survivor, somewhere deep within himself, throws an emotional switch. The "acceptable" person resurfaces, surveys the situation, and denies insidious anger its foothold—and an afternoon of depression ensues.

Depression is characterized by a sense of hopelessness, a desire to withdraw from everybody and everything, and a lack of response to stimulation. Depression can encompass many feelings, including self-pity, emptiness, and apathy. Its grip encloses the survivor in a tunnel of leaden despair. The feeble light at the end of this tunnel is too far away to matter, and must, it seems, be meant for others anyway. When in the state of depression, you feel, with complete conviction, that all life's castles are built on shifting sands. In fact, the only solid rocks in sight seem to hang like boulders from a chain around your neck. The slightest task seems monumental and meaningless, the smallest decision, baffling. While there are many who advocate taking life one day at a time, when in the grip of depression, it may be necessary to reduce that formula to a minute at a time: "I will make lunch and then see what happens," "I have succeeded in making lunch, so perhaps now I can manage to do the laundry." During states of depression, couples with happy marriages will make you miserable, and the sight of an older couple holding hands may trigger an evening of sorrow.

Sorrow too is a coat of many colors, such as sadness, loneliness, deprivation, and helplessness. If you don't spend the evening weeping over old photograph albums, you may spend it on the telephone, telling anyone who will listen about your love and your loss. When the hour becomes too late to disturb those happy friends and families, you may find yourself clinging once more to the late show for a little comfort and companionship. If you do finally sleep, you may be haunted by dreams or nightmares of sadness and pain.

A year after Joe's death, Susan dreamed about a strange and magical bird. She met him as she walked through a dense forest into a clearing of light. There, on the limb of a birch tree, perched the most beautiful bird in the world. Every feather on his small body was a different color, and his fragile frame displayed every hue and shade that has ever been seen. His brilliance cast an iridescent glow, and the gentle forest wind shifted and rearranged his colors in kaleidoscopic patterns.

"I am the Wing-scotter," said the bird, "and it is my fate to hold the most unbearable job on earth. Only those who know grief can know me," he continued, "for I am called only by those in anguish. I must fly wherever in the world there exists a human being in acute distress. The human, like you," he said to Susan, "may see me for a moment, but only to a rare few do I confide my purpose. Then, becoming invisible, I fly into the breast of that sad human, where I am destined to peck at his heart until I pierce it. It is at the moment of piercing that the human being feels his heart break within him."

Suddenly, the bird was gone. As Susan felt the tug at her heart begin, she awoke to face another day of grief.

This amazing sweep of emotions, from shock to anger to depression to sorrow, often constitutes just one more day of mourning. There are, however, other faces of grief, which are even more complex. In fact, the length of time it takes to complete grief's passage—which will enable you one day to step as a whole person, emotionally intact, into a new and fulfilling life—often depends on your pretraumatic personality, the person you were before the tragedy occurred.

For example, survivors with dependent personalities, who have never achieved real autonomy, may get lost in fear and helplessness, where they remain immobilized for months. Feelings of "I am nobody," "I am only half a person," and "I am completely empty" may prevail, making these individuals potential burdens on anyone who is close to them. Nor will narcissists be able to accept their losses easily; they will find it difficult to move past the How could this happen to me? stage. Those unable to face their anger will feel like acting it out, displacing anger in their rages at God, doctors, neighbors, and anyone unfortunate enough to be nearby. Those who have always had problems dealing with separation will suffer more and longer. Individuals whose fear of crying, pain, and suffering is so great that all these are avoided or suppressed may experience pathological mourning at a later date. In other words, if you have a strong negative self-image, you may have trouble growing through your grief without professional help.

Those who are mourning for a nonmarital companion have a different problem and a rugged path to travel. Besides the legal and economic confusion this situation almost inevitably creates, the mourning process itself is complicated. In addition to losing a loving partner, those who have chosen nontraditional life-styles are often denied the compassion, understanding, and support that are so crucial to progress through grief.

A difficult fact all grievers must learn is that although a person may die, a relationship does not. And since few relationships are completely resolved in life, the unresolved elements of a relationship live on long after a partner's death. Some survivors are trailed by the words they left unspoken.

Molly and Dave's relationship of fifty years didn't depend much on words. They nurtured each other quietly and were secure in their love. Each knew well the other's strengths and weaknesses, and each respected both. Molly knew that Dave hated to see her cry; the tears of one he loved so dearly made him feel miserable and helpless. Molly saved her tears for private moments.

When Dave became incurably ill and suffered long hours of pain, Molly did everything she could to help him. Knowing that their time together was short, Molly became filled with longing to tell Dave how very much she loved him. But she knew that if she tried to speak the words, she would be unable to control the tears behind them. Wishing to spare him her anguish, she remained silent. Today, four months after Dave's death, Molly still wishes desperately for one more chance to tell her husband of the depth of her abiding love.

Other survivors are pursued by the memories of angry words.

Joe was furious when he realized that there was nothing doctors or medicine could do to save his life. He felt cheated and outraged that he would not live to see his daughters grown. On some days he directed his anger at his daughters and at Susan, his wife, because he could not bear the thought that they would go on living without him. Two days before he died, he called Susan to the bedroom and recited to her a list of all the ways he felt she had ever failed him: the evening she didn't understand the seriousness of his problems at work, the time she laughed at him when he had such a bad cold. . . .

Although intellectually Susan understood Joe's anger, emotionally she was shattered. For years the echo of the words spoken that day resounded so loudly that the softer voices of better days could not be heard.

One day, four years after Joe's death, as Susan drove to the supermarket, she remembered an evening when she and Joe had watched a very funny television program. She remembered how together they had laughed so hard that they had doubled over, holding their stomachs and gasping for breath, until Joe had finally tumbled off the sofa onto the rug, where he lay exhausted, tears of laughter streaming down his face.

Susan laughed, too, all the way to the supermarket. She had finally forgiven him! She was beginning to be able to integrate the good times with the bad. She was beginning to see the relationship as a whole, with all its strengths and weaknesses, and to accept it as such.

Although friends inevitably underestimate the length of the grieving process, they can be very helpful during this period of pain and soul-searching. Rather than recycling them interminably in your head, it helps to have others with whom to share the meaning of your loss and the ways in which you now will have to change. The void created by the death of a spouse must be filled, and it is usually filled by many people—relatives, colleagues, neighbors, old friends. It is in this way, too, that the presence of a good support group can be valuable.

Support groups are based on a common bond of experience. Group members share three intertwined goals: to improve each other's emotional well-being, to help others, and to be helped in the process. Tremendous energy and power exist in such groups, and each member can benefit enormously from interaction with the others. Widowed people need to tell each other how much they are hurting; how confused, overwhelmed, insecure, and abandoned they feel; how empty life seems; and how frightened they are of facing the future alone. Because they are strangers to each other, members are able to share feelings that might be difficult or embarrassing to discuss with friends and relatives. The anonymity such groups provide allows for the expression of the ignoble side of grief. Furthermore, no member will ever tell you "Time heals" or "You're young; you'll marry again." And, because these people are at different points in their grief, you can get a good look at where you have been and how far you have progressed, while learning from veterans that hope and progress lie ahead. In fact, support group veterans often become role models for those less experienced, who are searching for direction.

Of course, good role models can be of invaluable assistance, no matter where you meet them. Talk to those who have survived loss and created new and different lives of purpose. Watch these gritty survivors and learn as much as you can from their experiences. Their insights can open new directions for you, and their successes can provide you with hope and inspiration. If they could do it, so can you.

You may find inspiration in friends who have never married. Grievers who have lived within a family framework often think only in terms of doing things for someone else; when the someone else is no longer there, actions suddenly feel barren and pointless.

One spring day while still deep in mourning, Susan went to her regular Thursday piano lesson. She was surprised to see a bowl of brightly colored Easter eggs on her teacher's living-room coffee table. Dale, a man in his seventies, had been a bachelor all his life. Thinking that they must have been a present from one of his students, Susan asked, "Where did you get the Easter eggs?"

"I went to the store, I bought 'em, and then I brought 'em home and dyed 'em," Dale replied with pride. "I like to eat them too!" he added enthusiastically.

Susan had trouble concentrating on the music that morning. As the stumbling notes of a Brahms intermezzo filled the cheerful yellow room, Susan's mind was occupied with the revolutionary idea that you could, on occasion, do something nice for yourself—just because you might enjoy it. Although Brahms suffered that morning, Susan stopped at the florist on her way home and bought a bunch of daffodils for the empty vase on her bedroom bureau.

While human beings who have traveled beyond the realm of your own experience can often serve as guideposts, there are other aids to recovery that lie beyond the human dimension. Those who have always felt that life holds real meaning will have an easier time with grief than those who view life as nothing more than an accident of nature. Those who nurture a faith in something beyond themselves—a force, a religion, God—will often find in their faith immeasurable comfort. The rituals that accompany religion may serve as a support; the traditional wake or shiva, for instance, encourages a brief period of intense mourning and publicly signifies that someone valuable has been lost.

However, faith is not to be confused with the clergy. While there are of course many outstanding members of the clergy who have been properly trained to deal with grief, there are also, unfortunately, many who are still untrained, who lack the skills that would enable them to become a constructive force in the process of healing. If you have turned to your clergyperson and come away empty-handed, try to separate your disappointment from your faith. Later, when you have found other avenues to aid you in your growth, you can perhaps help your church or synagogue in this department.

While friends, support groups, role models, and faith are important aids to recovery, you must never overlook the wisdom of your own inner voice. Somewhere deep inside of you lies the knowledge of how to heal yourself. Dig to uncover that wisdom and discard all advice, however well intentioned, that runs contrary to the dictates of your own nature. If your sister-in-law advises you to go home and face your grief by having a good cry on a night when you are unable to look at your grief sideways (let alone face it), pay no attention to her whatsoever and take yourself off to a movie or concert. Save her words for the day when you are better prepared to bear the weight of your loss. If your best friend insists that you come out of your shell and join the old gang at the bowling alley while you are in the process of an inward search that requires time alone, turn him down. Have patience with yourself when you do not measure up to the timetable of progress set by others, and never try to cut your path against your own grain.

Nine months after Marv died, Margaret was invited to join some friends for dinner and the theater. In the middle of her delicious meal, Margaret suddenly realized that the most direct route from the restaurant to the playhouse would take her past the very spot where the truck, colliding with Marv's car, had killed him. Margaret's appetite vanished, and she withdrew from conversation as her mind searched wildly for an escape from the ordeal now facing her. Should she explain that she had not been able to bring herself to pass that spot since the day of the accident? Should she feign illness and call for a taxi to take her home? Should she burst into tears?

Because she was still very fragile, Margaret was paralyzed. She acted on none of these options. Instead, she endured a shuddering ride as she fought to banish the image of the fatal crash from her mind. By the time this miserable evening drew to a close, Margaret had developed new respect for grief's tyrannical power, and for the strange and urgent knowledge her inner voice possessed.

Through the months that follow your loss, as you

attempt to listen to your needs beneath the ebb and flow of grief's emotions, you will begin, almost without realizing it, to develop the skills that will enable you to keep your head above a rising tide. During the early stages of grief, your skills may be focused on nothing more complicated than surviving just one more day.

Pat, a writer who works at home, found a way of tricking herself that worked well during the first grim months. Before she started her daily assignment, she would tell herself that whenever it became unbearable, she would simply get right back into bed and watch a soap opera. Pat would work for an hour or two and then present herself with the choice again: "I can go to bed now if I like, or I can continue to work." Well involved in her project at this point, she would invariably choose to continue with her work. In this manner, Pat managed to generate enough income to support herself and her daughter. She never did return to bed, and the heroes and heroines of the soaps were left to solve their problems without her silent support.

Pat was not denying her grief during these hours of work. She was, however, allowing her involvement with the the task at hand to provide her a temporary escape from the painful feelings.

As time went on, a regular schedule of work would become a daily habit for Pat, and habit can be a comforting phenomenon. The old habits—the familiar homey routines of married life—disappear with the death of a partner. New challenges present themselves each day, new responsibilities must be shouldered and decisions must be reached—decisions as simple as what to cook for dinner and as complicated as finding the right college for your teenager. And as you meet these challenges, new habits form unconsciously. When you have made it through one month, the next month will be a little easier. What was at first new and frightening gradually becomes familiar.

As responsibilities mount, controllers may have a bit of an edge over those who roll with the flow. Although initially controllers may be more stunned by the way fate has upset their neatly arranged applecarts, they will also be more anxious to get those apples back in place. Controllers are usually eager to take over the reins, thus beginning to steer their own courses once again. They are extremely uncomfortable when placed in the role of victim.

Margaret was miserable as, just three months after her husband's death, the day of their twentieth wedding anniversary approached. She was quite certain that the only way to deal with it would be to close the door, pull down the shades, and cry for twenty-four hours. She made plans to do just that. Then Margaret's friend Carolyn arrived from New Mexico, holding an armful of fuji chrysanthemums, the flowers of Margaret's wedding bouquet. Carolyn was disturbed by Margaret's game plan. Eventually she convinced Margaret that her children would have a hideous day too unless the family could be together for the anniversary.

The day dawned, the children were collected from four different places, lunch was consumed without tears, and the children were returned. By the end of the day, Margaret realized that taking charge and forming a plan when she saw a bad day coming made far more sense than simply lying there and letting it happen.

Those who roll with the flow may display a dangerous tendency to wallow. Rather than taking an active hand in their lives, they are apt to sit back and wait to see which card will be put on the table next. They run the risk of feeling at the mercy of fate and often lack the courage to trust their own instincts and needs.

There are dangers inherent in both the controller's and his opposite's philosophies. A controller must think twice before taking a radical step, since he's too apt to take any old step simply to avoid ambivalence. Controllers don't like swinging in the wind. A person who rolls with the flow needs to step out on a limb a bit and make a few decisions, until he realizes that he too can take a hand in the shaping of his dreams.

Regardless of type, sooner or later you will attend your first party alone. Alone, you will watch your child step forward and receive her diploma. You will go to your grandchild's band concert without your spouse beside you, joining in enthusiastic applause for little Tommy's trumpet solo. You will try to succeed in the accomplishment of the numerous daily tasks, previously performed by your mate, that make life run smoothly and comfortably. At a time when you are exhausted and miserable, you will be forced to tackle many new and strange challenges and to learn new skills. And at this point, when your self-confidence is precarious at best, your first attempts will not always succeed.

Lilly loved the opera and had had a subscription to it for years. The first time she attended a performance without her husband at her side, she was terrified. She wanted somehow to be able to see, hear, and enjoy the opera without having anyone notice that she was alone. Wishing to be invisible, she left her seat during the intermission and made her way to a dark corner, where she smoked three fast cigarettes. Then she started creeping back toward her seat, which was down a long staircase. But she tripped and fell down the entire length of carpeted stairs in the grand lobby of the Metropolitan Opera House, before a crowd of horrified operagoers. The first question those who scooped her up asked was "Who is here with you?"

Much of this chapter—and much of this book—is about trying, and trying again. Whether you are single or married, young or old, life requires that you make many attempts at the things that are important to you. It's just so much harder now, when you are emotionally bruised and battered. Even a first try at a new experience can be terrifying, and the temptation is to run in the opposite direction. Yet while attending a party by yourself may seem like an odious idea, if you make it through the first, you may find yourself enjoying the second and actually looking forward to the third. The first time the roof leaks and you realize with horror that it has to be replaced, you may hire some perfectly charming fellow who ends up making mincemeat of your rosebushes and then sends you a bill that is twice what you expected. Chalk it up to experience. The next time you need work done, you will be more shrewd—you'll ask for an estimate, and you won't pay a dime until the rosebushes are replaced.

In spite of life's demands, grief remains an inner struggle, requiring a ruthless examination of self, tremendous fortitude, and the courage to try again. Grief forces you to grow and change at the very moment when you most strongly desire to cling to your former self. Thrown out of the secure nest that formed your emotional home, and aching from that loss, you are asked to learn to fly. It can be done. The pain, which often threatens to make the effort impossible, will be lessened during the hours spent absorbed by your job or an abiding interest, and in the moments set aside for the chores and tasks that make daily survival possible.

There are other respites from grief too. Some of them may surprise you. The unexpected touch of a friend's hand may make you see with sudden clarity, the dearness of that friend and the meaning he or she brings to your life. Driving home one evening, you may be forced to pull over to the side of the road when the splendor of a sunset brings tears to your eyes. As you watch the sun disappear in purple, you may realize that until this moment you have never really taken the time to see and appreciate this miracle.

Moments like these make us aware that life itself is a great and glorious gift. In the wake of these rare moments, you may feel the first vague stirrings of concern over how to make the most of this gift. Although the direction your journey will take may not yet be clear, this concern will set your feet on its path. It is a path that can lead to a meaning and purpose unimagined in the days you once took for granted.

POINTS TO REMEMBER

1. Each passage through grief is as unique as the individual who experiences it; thus, your period of mourning will never be exactly like another's.

2. A familiarity with the stages and characteristics of grief will help you understand what to expect during this period, and on bad days it may help to reassure you that you are not losing your mind.

3. An intellectual comprehension of grief cannot replace the emotional experience of living through it. Be patient, and allow your emotions to catch up with your mind.

4. Expect reckless and chaotic mood swings, and realize that although each intense emotion may feel as if it has settled in to stay forever, this too will pass.

5. If your pregrief self-image was a poor one, do not hesitate to seek professional help during this stressful period; allow yourself this opportunity for growth.

6. Although a person dies, the relationship with that person does not.

7. Work toward an honest and realistic acceptance of the strengths and weaknesses of your relationship.

8. As you struggle to determine who you are without your spouse, share this process of discovery with friends, allowing them to add their perceptions to your growth.

9. Consider joining a support group if a good one is available in your area.

10. Seek out widows and widowers who have moved beyond the period of mourning, and learn all you can from them.

11. Scrutinize the lives of others you admire, perhaps those who are living alone.

12. If you have faith in something beyond yourself, turn to it, and do not confuse disappointment in individuals such as clergy with disappointment in God.

13. Never overlook the wisdom of your own inner voice, which will tell you what you need. Ignore all outside advice that disregards those needs.

14. Don't measure your progress according to anyone else's timetable.

15. Make plans for difficult days, such as anniversaries and holidays. Take charge of these dangerous hours and avoid despair.

16. If you are a controller by nature, think twice before taking radical steps and discuss major decisions with wise friends.

17. If you are inclined to roll with the flow, learn to trust your instincts, and dare to make the decisions that will change your life for the better.

18. If at first you don't succeed at mastering the many new challenges that face you, try, try again.

19. Venture out into life; don't let fear hold you back. What at first feels strange and uncomfortable may turn into fun.

20. Try to grow more aware of the gift of life, and heed your inclinations toward responsibility to that gift.

5 | The Family in Crisis

The effect of order within the family is to create an influence that brings order into the world: It is achieved when the head of the family has substance in his words . . . . and duration in his way of life.
— The I Ching or Book of Changes

*T*he undertaker was right on time, but Lisa's household was in shambles. Friends had unexpectedly arrived just moments before, and one of them, recalling the last glorious fishing trip with Lisa's late husband, Dan, wept inconsolably as he sat at the end of the large kitchen table. (Unknowingly, he had selected Dan's chair.) Lisa's six-year-old daughter, Jennifer, unable to cope any longer with the tears of her parents' friends, retreated to a corner with two of her dolls, whom she engaged in a loud and raucous game *of "house." Meanwhile, Jennifer's three- and four-year-old brothers paid tribute to the gravity of the occasion by marching around the house to the beat of toy drums, pausing solemnly at regular intervals in the kitchen doorway to chant, "Daddy's dead, Daddy's dead." As the undertaker, speaking over the din, attempted to question Lisa regarding her wishes for her husband's burial, Lisa's mother, hoping to spare her daughter some painful decisions, answered each of his questions with a description of the fitting propriety of her own husband's funeral. The undertaker remained unruffled; he'd seen it all before.*

The loss of one of its members throws a family into crisis. To understand the enormous stress a mortal blow inflicts on the family as a whole—and on each of its members as well—it is helpful to consider the family's functioning methods during more routine times. The healthy, unstressed family operates under certain systems. Each member in the system is related, by both heredity and emotion, to each of the other members, and each member is crucial to the family's organization and balanced functioning powers. The family unit provides protection and sustenance to its members and gives a sense of belonging and togetherness. Each member finds his own identity within this unit and realizes that he is a separate individual.

A death disrupts the delicate balance between the family's togetherness and its members' individuality. The lost parent held a specific role, important to the family structure. Eventually, the remaining family members will assume these responsibilities, the surviving parent taking on those obligations that require an adult's experience and the children filling in with those abilities that are in keeping with their ages and development. Until this occurs, though, the positions are altered, and the family's normal patterns of transaction are short-circuited. Before new and successful patterns can be established, each family member must make significant adjustments, changing not only his role as a family member but his relationship to every other family member as well. This is not a step easily taken in the midst of suffering. Pain creates desperate need, and in the shadow of death, family members cling to one another, offering the comfort of their mutual love. In the weeks that follow loss, the family members' essential love for one another sustains and encourages them. But the temptation to smother a fragile sister or an aching father with attention is great, and unremitting comfort can become stifling.

Before the construction of new roles can begin, each person needs time and space to absorb the loss in his own way. All family members must maintain the ability to disengage, when necessary, from the unit. But disengagement can be carried too far. Sometimes consideration for another's need for privacy may lead family members to construct impenetrable walls around the areas of their grief—so as "not to upset Mom," for instance. When this happens, the family's balance dips dangerously toward too much individual isolation.

Given these ideas, let's take a closer look at the problems confronting Lisa's family on the afternoon of the undertaker's visit.

Before the undertaker had even rung the doorbell, an adjustment of family roles had been forced by the arrival of Dan's inconsolable friend. The friend's unchecked sorrow made the family members feel as if they should put aside their own despair to comfort him. While a low-keyed exchange of shared grief is consoling, a "sympathy" call in which the sympathizer's sorrow upstages the grief of the deceased's immediate family is not constructive.

Six-year-old Jennifer reacted to the visitor angrily. This man not only had usurped her father's place at the head of the table but had successfully engaged the attention of her mother, thus blocking Jennifer's normal pattern of running to her mother when confronted with hurt or fear. By the time the undertaker arrived on the scene, creating further demands on her mother's time and focus, Jennifer felt that her own grief and confusion would remain unnoticed. Defiantly, she disengaged from the family circle and, turning to her dolls, attempted to drown out the terrifying ramifications of her father's death by constructing a very vocal game about a much more stable house.

Jennifer's younger brothers, however, persisted in the hope of winning attention—if not their mother's, almost anybody's would do. Something of great importance had taken place, and they had learned that the attention-getting words were "Daddy's dead." Eager to maintain togetherness during this day of obvious significance for their family, they marched like town criers from room to room, creating for themselves roles of import and prestige. When even doting Grandma failed to respond, their chant rose in pitch.

Grandma, however, was completely absorbed at that moment by her panic at her own growing responsibilities. Until the day of Lisa's marriage, she and her late husband had been Lisa's providers and caretakers. Had Dan's death, Grandma wondered, thrust the well-being of this entire family back into her lap? As she smothered Lisa's initiative to take charge of the burial arrangements for her husband, Grandma fought to repress the guilt-ridden resistance she felt toward this new and overwhelming burden. If she had been able to read her daughter's mind, she would have been surprised, hurt, and perhaps a bit relieved to discover Lisa's seething resentment of her mother's well-intended intervention.

Lisa was furious and astounded. What did her mother think she was doing? Dan was *her* husband, and all the choices regarding his funeral were hers alone. How dare her mother try to take this last gesture from her? But Lisa, too, feared that, now that she was no longer a wife, she would regress to her role as rebellious adolescent daughter. Intent on interrupting her mother's seemingly mindless interference, and aware that Dan's friend still awaited her attentions, Lisa knew she'd have to confront her own and her children's feelings later. Beneath these frustrations, however, lay the grim fact that, when the sun set on this difficult day, there would be no familiar comforting arms, no words of consolation from the voice she longed most to hear. I need time alone, she thought. I need time enough to remember everything about him.

Lisa and her family were miserable and at odds with one another. Private needs and perceptions governed individual words and actions, and the family cohesiveness which normally operated during times of outside threat, was clearly lacking.

Confronted with grief, family members are caught between the pull of sympathy for another's loss and the egotistical needs of their own bereavement.

Shortly after his mother's death, nine-year-old Jeff, pained by his father's need for seclusion, shouted, "You've lost a wife, but you can get another. I can never get another mother!"

While the family suffers a collective loss, it must not be forgotten that each individual of that family now stands at the center of his or her own private tragedy. For the rest of his life, Jeff will recall in painful detail the events of the day he lost his mother. Jeff's father will for years seek someone with whom he can share the warm moments that made his marriage so special.

As family members search for the means of coping with their private tragedies (all the while reminding themselves that the person in the next room is facing equal loss), together they remain acutely sensitive to the void created by death. Reminders are everywhere. On a bedside table, a book still lies open to the last page she read. Behind a closet door hang the clothes he will never wear again. At dinner, the family averts its eyes from the empty chair that tells the same sad story night after night.

When Susan learned that Joe was dying, she used to try to imagine what it would be like to sit with her girls at the dining-room table without him. In her mind, she pictured her daughters running to the "dinner's ready" call.

"What are we having?" they would shout.

"Spaghetti," she would reply, knowing it was a favorite.

They would all sit down, and then the silent, hateful chair would face them. "How will we ever be able to eat a bite?" she wondered, months before Joe had even left them.

When a family is confronted by a too-painful emptiness, some of its members may attempt to fill the aching void.

Almost immediately after Marv's death, Margaret's sixteen-

*year-old confided to all who would listen: "I just won't go to college.
I will work and support the family."*

An eldest child is apt to be especially susceptible to a
self-defeating compulsion to assume the lost parent's role.
And because it is so very lonely at the top, a surviving parent
often unconsciously encourages this impossible dream. If you
are a sole surviving parent, attempt to protect your children
from taking on the decisions and responsibilities that once
belonged to your partner. While it is appropriate and even
commendable to ask a twelve-year-old, "What movie shall
we see?" or "Shall we order mushrooms on our pizza?" it is
entirely inappropriate to expect a twelve-year-old to assume
the responsibility of selecting a vacation spot or a new living-
room rug.

Adult children may be particularly vulnerable to the
slightest and subtlest requests for help.

*After a year of widowhood, many areas of Jane's life were
going well, and her moments of helplessness were less frequent.
However, there was one persistent problem. Don, her twenty-three-
year-old son, had dropped out of college. Although he attempted
stints at various jobs, he was fired routinely because of his uncontrollable temper. Things became more difficult as he refused to adhere
to his curfew and adopted a defiant attitude that completely disrupted
Jane's life and the lives of his two younger siblings.*

*Jane approached Lilly for help. As she described the situation,
she mentioned that in the past year utility bills and insurance pre-
miums had occasionally disappeared from her desk. When she investigated their whereabouts, Don confessed to taking them and paying
them on his own.*

*Lilly immediately recognized that this problem was not only
Don's but Jane's as well. She gently suggested that Jane's occasional
helplessness unwittingly gave Don the message that she expected
him to be the new head of the family. Although Don was unable to
identify the source of his tension, he might, Lilly counseled, feel
panicked and angry at the prospect of trying to fill his father's shoes.*

*This was the last thing Jane wanted, either for herself or for
Don. She was proud of the areas in which she had assumed leadership of her family. She had gained much confidence through making*

many large and small decisions that had proven beneficial to her family's welfare.

Jane needed to take a step back in order to see how her actions had misled her son. She saw that when feeling helpless, she had comforted herself by telling her worries to Don.

Jane's insight wasn't acquired overnight. But several weeks of difficult introspection, guided by an objective outsider (in this case, a therapist), led her to an ever-deepening understanding of Don's problem. Jane decided to share future moments of helplessness with close friends. She then reestablished control of her mail and discussed with Don those responsibilities that fell in his domain and those that didn't. Their discussion relieved Don of the burdens of inappropriate responsibility and allowed him to regain his rightful position as the family's eldest child.

A parent's obligation to protect a child's rightful position doesn't end at some neatly delineated point.

Two days after Lilly's husband died, she sat down to talk with her daughter, Susan, a young woman who had recently accepted a good job in another city.

"At some point," Lilly cautioned, blinking back tears, "someone may suggest that you give up your job and move back here so that I can have you close to me. I would like to have you here, but don't do it."

"Mother," her daughter interrupted, "someone has already suggested it."

Lilly knew that, although the temptation to bond an adult child into the place of the lost spouse can be great, it is not a substitution that works for either the surviving mate or the child.

Of course, no sooner do you get one child moving in the right direction than another, who seemed to be doing so well, suddenly veers toward a cliff. This characteristic of grief is particularly noticeable in large families, in which the gaps between stages of development must be bridged by many members simultaneously. When you have succeeded in heading off one child's attempt to take total charge of the discipline of his younger siblings, for instance, you may look up to see another tackling her schoolwork with newfound maturity while a third takes a drastic nosedive back to the days when she had to be right by your side. In grieving families, new paths of transaction often coexist with disintegrating boundaries of individuality.

When Andy's father died, he felt parentless. The only son in a large family of girls, Andy had formed a relationship with his father that excluded both his sisters and his mother. Fortunately, in the weeks that followed the death, Andy's mother was able to see beyond her own grief and perceive her son's need. Tentatively at first, then more confidently, mother and son grew into a new, stronger relationship.

However, Lizzie, the youngest child, who had been looking forward to going away to school, became increasingly apprehensive about this move. Although Lizzie's mother was able to maintain the boundaries that would allow this daughter to leave, Lizzie held on to her past, fearing it would be lost if she allowed herself to grow beyond it.

Lone parents must keep an unceasingly wary lookout for stumbling blocks in the paths of their families' development. They must seek to protect the growth and individuality of family members. They must hold fast to the resiliency that will enable them to support and encourage those who, now more than ever, need the understanding and direction a caring parent can provide.

Relationships, both within and without the family, change when a family member dies. As months and years pass and the children grow and mature, relationships and boundaries must be redefined and rearranged accordingly. When a lone, hurting parent assumes responsibility for the family's welfare, he or she inspires all its members to relate to one another through love, and to grow.

When a surviving parent is desperate with grief over the loss of a mate, the weight of total responsibility for an entire family's welfare often seems too heavy to carry.

In the weeks following Joe's death, Susan became increasingly fearful that she would disappoint her children. She had been the disciplinarian of the family; Joe had been the conspiratorial playmate. Susan supervised bedtime procedure while Joe passed around the lemon drops. As her grief grew, Susan became convinced that her daughters, if they had been forced to choose, would have opted for her death and Joe's survival.

As she had suspected, the hours at the dinner table were the most difficult. It was there that the empty chair seemed to speak so eloquently of Joe's absent zest. It was there that she most doubted her ability to guide and nourish her children's lives. Susan began to try to imagine evenings in which they would share their daily experiences with laughter again. Although she didn't realize it at the time, she had established a goal that she would begin to strive for.

Most single parents are familiar with the feelings of inadequacy that accompany the complex problems presented by raising children. (As a matter of fact, these same feelings are not uncommon in two-parent households!) It is extremely important that those who now seek to aid the lone parent do all they can to foster this survivor's confidence in his or her abilities to cope with the tasks at hand. Grandparents, for instance, must avoid the pitfall of viewing their bereaved adult offspring as children.

Grandparents, too, become confused and unsure of themselves in the process of redefining their roles. Watching a son or daughter through the loss of a mate is heart wrenching, and the inability to put things right again (with a kiss or an ice-cream cone, as in the good old days) is frustrating. Like Lisa's mother, many grandparents, when confronted with the death of a son-in-law or daughter-in-law, overcompensate for the loss by reassuming parental control, an act that eventually undermines the authority of their adult child.

Two days after her husband's funeral, Elaine drove her mother to the airport. With tears in her eyes, she hugged her mother and thanked her for her help.

"There's just one little thing I'd like to mention," her mother said, as she twisted and untwisted the strap of her pocketbook. She took a deep breath. "Think of your children, dear, and don't be promiscuous!" she blurted out, and disappeared into the crowd.

The regression of a bereaved adult to an outdated role is compounded if the adult continually turns to his parents when disciplining the children or making decisions. Here again, while it is undoubtedly appropriate to ask Grandma if she wants mushrooms on the pizza, the choice of a living-room rug is not a decision she should be asked to make.

A single parent cannot be both mother and father to his or her children, and any attempt to assume both roles is doomed to eventual failure. However, the surviving parent can be a caring, nurturing father or mother and can and should accept, as quickly as possible, his or her inherited responsibilities as sole head of the household. When they encourage this effort, grandparents provide the best possible support.

The threat to the balance of the family's structure does not necessarily diminish in the case of an older surviving spouse whose parents are no longer living. Now it is the adult children, long established in homes of their own, who, worried about his or her welfare, may seek to take command of their bereaved parent's life. Even the best-intentioned adult children are often tempted to try to fill the place of the deceased parent. The desolate remaining parent may be all too tempted to allow this to happen.

Dorothy was an extraordinarily attractive woman with a satisfying job through which she met many new people. When she became a widow, she was grateful that her two sons and their families lived close by. During the days of darkest grief, their loving care supported her. Finding weekends too lonely to bear, Dorothy began spending them at the homes of her sons, alternating families each week. During these visits, the hosting son took charge of Dorothy's bookkeeping, household maintenance, and other responsibilities that had formerly belonged to Dorothy's husband. This pattern continued until Lilly, spotting it, suggested that it had trapped the very capable Dorothy in quite a peculiar bind.

Instead of teaching Dorothy to take charge of her life (not to mention her bookkeeping), her overly considerate sons had taken charge of it themselves. Instead of gently encouraging her to develop an active social life, they had provided one. While this type of support might have been appropriate for a very aged or infirm parent, it was not what Dorothy needed. Dorothy's sons, in a sincere effort to help, had aided their mother's dependence at a time when independence would have fostered growth.

To survive successfully, the bereaved adult must be willing to shoulder the responsibility for the quality of his own life. This requires the ability to make decisions, and, in the case of the survivor with dependents, it requires the strength and wisdom to be a leader. Even when you realize that repeated dependence on parents or offspring can further undermine the weakened family structure, this burden can seem so lonely that it appears unbearable.

Margaret found that friends were invaluable allies at this time. She found that different friends had strengths in different areas. By her willingness to ask advice, Margaret was able to use these friends' various strengths to help her choose between the confusing options facing her. Through these discussions, Margaret learned much about the decision-making process, and because she refrained from placing responsibility for her choices in anyone else's hands, she was able to assume and maintain control of her household. In time, as she became more familiar with her role as commander in chief, she could look back in astonishment at the many small decisions she had made on her own each day. Her confidence in her ability to make even the tougher choices grew.

You are making family decisions, both large and small, each day. If a decision proves wrong, a new one can be reached. The nice thing about mistakes, after all, is that they can be corrected. Remember that. If, despite corrections, family development seems to be blocked, the experienced eye of a counselor (or even a wise and honest friend) may help to illuminate the problem. Little by little, as decisions are amended and impediments removed, families initially devastated by loss may find that they have used this crisis as a stepping-stone to deepened affection and widened avenues of understanding. One day, they may even be surprised by the sudden realization that they are actually able to enjoy themselves again.

Months after Joe's death, Kimberly announced that her fifth-grade class would soon be starting a course in sex education.

"We each received a booklet about it. But Mom," she exclaimed, "I think I already know more about it than they do!"

"What makes you think so?" Susan asked.

"Well," Kim explained, "this booklet is entitled 'Getting to Know Your Body,' but it has a picture of a horse on its cover!" She burst into giggles.

"A horse on the cover," little Amanda gasped, laughing hysterically without really knowing why.

"Do they think you're built like a horse, Kim?" Eva, who had a more sophisticated grasp of the issue, shouted.

The whole family laughed until the table shook.

POINTS TO REMEMBER

1. When a parent dies, the entire family experiences a period of upheaval as the comfortable patterns of transaction between its members are disrupted.
2. In order to establish new, successful patterns of transaction, each individual in the family must adjust his own role and relationship to every other member.
3. Recognize that during the beginning weeks of grief the individual needs of family members may disrupt the family's ability to function successfully as a unit.
4. Individual griefs progress to different levels at different times. Family members must look beyond the walls of personal loss if understanding within the family is to be achieved.
5. Remember that each member of a family that has experienced a death sees himself at the center of that loss. Each individual lives through his own private tragedy.
6. Recognize the need for a good balance between family togetherness and individual freedoms.
7. Learn to respond to family members' needs without suffocating the needy individual.
8. Be aware that too much dependence between family members can destroy the boundaries that protect individual growth.
9. Allow each individual the scope to absorb the loss in his own way and time.

10. Do not, however, let the walls between individuals grow insurmountably high. Don't respect privacy at the cost of the necessary sharing of grief.

11. Realize that children (particularly the eldest child) may feel compelled to try to assume the role of the lost parent.

12. Protect your children from taking on inappropriate responsibility.

13. Remember that if you are reluctant to make the decisions that will protect your family's welfare, your parents—or even your children—may seek to make them for you.

14. Hasten the redevelopment of family cohesiveness by accepting your role as your family's leader and the responsibilities that once belonged to your partner.

15. If you are the parent of a bereaved adult with dependent children, allow your child the space to assume control of his life and responsibility for the family. If you are the adult child of a widowed parent, allow your parent that same space.

16. If you are a sole surviving parent, discuss difficult decisions with knowledgeable friends instead of placing inappropriate responsibility on family members.

17. Learn all you can during these discussions about the decision-making process so that eventually you can handle difficult choices on your own.

18. Recognize that as children grow from one stage of maturation to another, family relationships and boundaries must be redefined accordingly.

19. If you have made decisions for your family that aren't working as you hoped they might, try to recognize and correct them.

20. Set your sights on the goals you hoped to achieve, and know that, with patience, they can be realized.

6 | Youthful Woes, Youthful Wonders: The Readjustment of the Child

When I was a child, I spake as a child, I understood as a child, I thought as a child: but when I became a man, I put away childish things.
—I CORINTHIANS 13:11

When left alone with his children, the surviving parent is, at some point, lightning-struck by an awareness of the frailty of his young. He (or she) may wish to hold them close. He may search for words to ease their pain. But before those words can be uttered, he may well be interrupted by the cheerful request: "Daddy, can we go out and play now?" Children, one psychologist noted, have short attention spans for sadness.

Children, like adults, experience grief's wasteland of

shock, numbness, panic, disorganization, and despair. Unlike adults, however, they dart in and out of the chaos. Children know that the loss of a parent must irrevocably alter the rest of their lives, and they are frightened by the powerful feelings accompanying this radical change. When the fright becomes too strong, a child may turn to a dollhouse or baseball diamond for distraction.

Each child is different; each child mourns in his own way. But all children mourn differently than adults, and it is extremely important that the parent understand this. Trusted adults must not try to rush a child into feeling better too soon. They must also refrain from goading him or her into sorrow when exuberance has granted a temporary respite from pain. Furthermore, they must strive to keep the lines of communication open, watching carefully for the warning signs of misunderstanding which may indicate that the child has somehow assumed responsibility for his parent's death.

All children deserve the dignity of grieving by their own timetables, reworking the experience of loss at different ages and stages of development until they can successfully integrate the values of the deceased parent into the rest of their lives. How the reality of loss affects the direction of the rest of their lives will be determined by their own personalities, by how much else they lose, and by the adequacy of the surrogates in their lives. But how children respond initially to the death of a parent depends on their resilience, relationship with the parent who has died, relationship with the remaining parent, and developmental age when the death occurs.

Preadolescent children respond to death in age-appropriate ways. It is helpful if surviving parents recognize and understand the normal responses of children who experience the death of a provider before they are old enough to provide for themselves.

Because an individual's perception of death is based on the wisdom of experience acquired in his years on the earth, children with little life experience will tend to pattern their behavior on the attitudes of those around them. The mother who weeps for days on end, all the while explaining how happy Daddy is in Heaven, presents her children with the choice between altruistic happiness for their daddy or misery for their mother and themselves. Parents who are uncomfortable expressing their emotions may teach their small children to view sorrow as a weakness, better hidden than acknowledged. However, even parents who are able to live with the pain without falling apart may discover that their young children have mirrored them so successfully that they appear to understand far more than they actually do.

Four-year-old Mimi attended her father's funeral. For weeks afterward, she watched her family weep. On special days she accompanied her mother to the cemetery and placed the flowers she had picked on her father's grave. Then one evening several months later, Mimi interrupted her bedtime story with the firm statement: "Daddy has been dead long enough. I want him back now."

Despite all the grief around her, Mimi clearly believed that death, like sleeping, was reversible. For months she had been waiting for a Rip Van Winkle ending. Why, she had wondered, did her mother not stop crying, wake her Daddy up, and get him out of that hole in the ground before winter snows fell?

Your young children may be confused on many fronts. Very young children do not easily distinguish animate beings from inanimate objects. They perceive themselves and their surroundings as immortal and immutable. They are the center of their worlds, and, while they think they can control all the good things that happen to them, they also (in spite of what they say to the contrary) take responsibility for the disasters. This reasoning process can result in the alarming conclusion "I was mad at Mom, and then she died." If the error of this cause and effect judgment is not exposed and corrected, it can haunt a child for the rest of his life. It is up to the grieving parent to convince this child that the loss is not his fault. The parent unable to do so should seek professional help.

A year and a half after his father's death in a car accident, Pete was still so absorbed in grief that he was unable to cope with second grade. He joined a group for bereaved children. It took weeks of listening to the experiences of others before Pete was able to reveal his belief that he had caused his father's death.

How? By washing the car on the morning of the accident. Pete had spent almost two years living with this unspeakable guilt. He was convinced that by inadvertently splashing water into the engine he had caused his father's car to malfunction and crash.

Six-year-olds have a very limited perspective of the world. "Very old people die," most six-year-olds have learned, and they have basked in the comfort of their youth. When this "truth" is turned upside down by the death of a not-so-old parent, they begin to question the other truths of their lives, and their worlds start to wobble.

Seven- to ten-year-olds, who are developing an intense curiosity about the way things work, may seem morbidly interested in death as they bombard their horrified parent with questions such as "What will Daddy's body look like after it's been in the ground for a year?" They may nonchalantly explain to friends, "My mom's in the ground decaying," or quite without thinking about it drop the casual remark "I wish I was dead."

As a child grows and acquires knowledge from birth to adolescence, his response to death is adjusted and expanded accordingly.

When Leslie was five, she lost her two grandparents in quick succession. Both grandparents had been closely involved in the daily life of her family. Except for one brief teary spell, Leslie's response to these important deaths was mainly one of denial. She put aside her feelings of loss and went on with her childhood.

At age eight, however, when her pet mouse died, Leslie entered into a very real grieving process, complete with dreams of her mouse, an idealization of their relationship, and a horrified reaction to the suggestion of a substitute. Leslie's troubled parents questioned her about the difference between her response to her grandparents' deaths and her reaction to her pet's demise and found that the intervening years of growth had quite clearly expanded Leslie's view of relationships and the void that their loss can leave behind.

All children dislike being thought of as different. "That

poor child whose mother died last year" is a demeaning label that, to a child's ear, smacks of freakishness. The Mother-Daughter Fashion Show and the Father–Son Picnic can provoke weeks of anguished anticipation in the bereaved child who will not attend these events.

Matthew spent one very long afternoon with his second-grade class painting a necktie rack and painstakingly drawing a Father's Day card. Although his father had been dead for three months, Matthew could not bear to sit idly, separated from his classmates by his loss. On the way home from school, Matthew tossed his gift into a neighbor's garbage can.

This type of problem doesn't have to develop. Had the teacher been alerted to Matthew's understandable sensitivity, she or he could have privately suggested a surprise necktie rack for Grandpa or Uncle Tom.

Other children may add a splash of personal flamboyance to the "poor child" label.

Seven-year-old Emily didn't like carrying her paper bag lunch to school. So each morning she dutifully took it from her mother and carried it down the long hill and around the corner, where before the bus came she discreetly fed it to her two delighted dogs.

When lunchtime arrived, Emily turned sadly to her friend Kristen. "My mother didn't make me any lunch again today," she sighed. Generous Kristen offered Emily half of her sandwich.

When Kristen went home and told her mother of Emily's woeful plight, Kristen's mother called the principal and magnanimously offered to make two lunches every morning, one for Kristen and one for "poor Emily."

The next morning, the principal called Emily into his office. "Why don't you bring a lunch to school?" he asked her kindly.

"My father is dead," Emily solemnly replied, looking him straight in the eye, "and my mother is too poor to buy us any food."

That afternoon the principal called Emily's mother. Mom took Emily shopping and let her pick out the flashiest lunch box in the five-and-dime store. Emily went to school the next day with a new image. Just one short lunch hour later, she became known to her friends as the lucky girl with the brand-new lunch box, and "poor Emily" disappeared.

After a death all children become concerned with their own safety; the younger the child, the greater his concern will be. Maintaining order and continuity can help. A mother who—whether in compassion or loneliness—suddenly suggests that little Joanie may now wish to sleep with her each night reinforces fears of new disasters and disrupts the familiar routines that, because they are familiar, provide security. The grieving child has more than enough fears already. "What will happen to me now?" "Who will take care of me?" and "How will I get what I need?" are normal, common worries of the child not yet able to care for himself.

Eight-year-old Edward became a hero when he pulled his floundering mother to the side of the pool, called for help, and kept her afloat until aid arrived. When asked where he had acquired the knowledge and strength to respond so quickly to this emergency, he replied: "I couldn't let anything happen to her. There'd be no one left to take care of me."

Central to all children's sense of safety is the knowledge that the remaining parent will not abandon them. Families diminished by a sudden death are especially vulnerable to the Who will be taken next? tremors.

Within days of Marv's death, Margaret's daughter Amy found herself unable to say the word good-bye. *"See you later," she would call to any departing member of her family. "Come back soon!"*

But Amy wasn't the only one with a problem. Soon this insidious anxiety spread like January's flu virus, until the entire family was afflicted. The leave-taking of any one of them for any reason struck terror in the hearts of those who awaited his or her return.

They began to attempt to reassure one another. "I'm going to the store," one of them would explain. "I'll be back in twenty-five or thirty minutes. Actually, it'll probably be closer to twenty-seven minutes, but don't worry if I'm a little late."

Gradually, each became aware of his or her own separation anxiety by watching the others' behavior. A discussion of their common problem comforted them.

The fear of abandonment can pose a very real threat to the child whose parent cannot see beyond her or his own grief and fear.

With four small children who needed her, Barbara grieved with very little privacy. Although she tried for their sakes to hold back her tears, she was lost for weeks in despair.

One day she received a laboriously written note from her seven-year-old: "Please, Mommy, come back," it read. "I don't know that you are you. You never smile anymore."

Many children, particularly adolescents, feel upset and threatened by a parent's grief. The adolescent, in a fierce struggle to achieve independence, sometimes seeks to steer not only her own course but her family's too. She wants her family to grieve when she feels like grieving, although she is apt to become highly indignant if they don't behave "normally" (or even gaily) on the afternoons her friends drop by. Teetering on the brink of adult responsibility, the adolescent, who desperately wants to believe that the world is manageable, may attempt to reject completely the vulnerability and frailty of his grieving parent. "Why are you always crying? I can't stand coming home to someone who is always sad," are the thoughts often expressed by the young woman or man who so intensely wants to view the world as a safe place in which happy endings can come true. This resistance to family grief lasts until the moment when this almost grown-up individual is suddenly and overwhelmingly undone by his or her own grief and tears. (Resistance may be resumed with alarming alacrity, however, when the outburst has passed.)

It is when the threat to a child's security is greatest that the charge "I wish you had died instead of Mom/Dad," is most likely to be spoken or implied. Needless to say, a remark of this nature is the very last thing an already miserable parent wishes to hear. It is helpful for grieving parents to understand that this charge is often a veiled plea for stability.

Unfortunately, bereaved parents may be so enclosed in their own terrors that they mistake a child's fears of instability for rejection, compounding the strain.

Gary didn't understand his teenage daughters, and they didn't seem to understand him. Just weeks after their mother's death, Susie's only interest in life seemed to be the tryouts for the cheerleading team, while Nancy hadn't spoken to her father since the day he vetoed her suggestion of a slumber party.

Puzzled and hurt, Gary stocked his freezer with TV dinners and took his Scotch to the bedroom, where he could watch the news in peace. After just a few drinks he'd be able to sleep. In time this pattern became a habit. Today, with hindsight, Gary realizes that his daughters lost him, as surely as they had lost their mother, at the time they needed him most.

Caring for children is a responsibility that doesn't end each day at five o'clock. There is no hour when you can lean back and safely conclude that your duties are finished, that all is under control. (When raising children, the feeling that everything's under control should always be considered a warning!) The parent, usually the father, unaccustomed to the demands of child rearing may be confounded by the never-ending complexities of the lives now in his or her care.

When Paul's wife was killed in an accident, he discovered almost immediately that he did not have the skills that would enable him to provide a safe and comfortable home for his seven-year-old daughter, Mattie. Paul didn't have a clue as to how to register a child in school, much less run a household. It was difficult for him to prioritize needs: musts, shoulds, and likes scrambled together as he attempted to establish guidelines for Mattie.

It took Paul some time to distinguish his own standards from those he'd inherited from his wife, and to work out a balance between his and Mattie's needs. In an attempt to cope, Paul allowed a number of kind and well-meaning women to enter his life and assume a role in his daughter's upbringing. It was not, however, until he took responsibility as the consistent care giver that he was rewarded with Mattie's trust and confidence. Not until Mattie became a teenager did Paul gain the satisfaction that every nurturing father deserves.

As surprising as it may seem, another stumbling block in the grieving parent's path is undisciplined compassion. The adult whose own parents are still alive is especially susceptible. He may stare in amazement at the loss his motherless children have sustained, or shake his fist at the sky in anger at life's arbitrary cruelty. He may attempt to overcompensate his children for their loss, creating, in the process, little monsters.

A number of parents of school-aged children met with Lilly to discuss this dilemma and its impact on their finances.

Steve began by explaining how, in the weeks following his wife's death, he could hardly bear his daughter Kate's sorrow. In an attempt to rekindle the light in her eyes, he began bringing home a few surprises. First it was the designer jeans she'd longed for; then, a goose-down jacket, just like the one she'd so admired on her friend Beverly. Next, he took her shopping for the faddish watch that all the girls were wearing: "But, Daddy, everybody has one!" Kate's whims became his command, but the light in her eyes did not return.

When Kate decided that she no longer liked the new watch she had chosen and requested another, Steve began to have misgivings. He denied her request. A few weeks later, when Steve bought himself a couple of shirts, Kate was furious. "Do you mean you can buy yourself shirts whenever you feel like it, and you can't afford to buy me one little watch?" she asked. Her outraged tone was that of a wife who can't afford pot roast because of her husband's extravagances. (An only child is particularly susceptible to taking over the departed parent's role.)

As Steve spoke, the other group members began nodding their heads in acknowledgment. When his tale concluded, all eyes turned to Lilly.

"The line between parent and child must be clearly defined," Lilly responded. "Your children should be provided with a realistic picture of the family's financial situation. They should be informed that Social Security is contributing to their support with monies that go directly into the family pot. But you are the parent, and it is your wisdom and experience that must determine how the household resources are spent. That is your responsibility. If you were to pass these decisions on to someone else, you would be shirking that responsibility. The needs of each member of the household must be

met," Lilly counseled, "and meeting your own needs should be no cause for guilt."

"The very same thing happened to me," Polly exclaimed. "When my birthday and wedding anniversary approached, I gave myself a present; I bought myself a ring. 'You bought yourself a ring?' my daughter asked incredulously."

Polly chuckled. "I just looked her straight in the eye and said, 'Yup. And I bought a pair of earrings, too!' "

There are many family responsibilities and decisions that can be shared. While the remaining parent must assume the role of chief, children should participate in the reallocation of tasks and chores. The parent must take the lead in these negotiations, gently confirming the somber reality that now confronts the family despite everyone's wishes to the contrary. "Yes," Dad must say to Jimmy, "you will be responsible for taking care of Billy after school today. Mom is not here to do that, and your help will be important to us all."

Ways of dealing with the empty chair at the end of the table (symbolic of the empty spot in each heart) must be developed too, and children should have a say in this process. (Everyone can take turns sitting in it; the chair can be moved; the table can be repositioned.) Each time a decision is reached, the family traditions shift, establishing the new ground in which different memories will grow. The new family history will be happier if all members have contributed to its growth.

Some of the most difficult decisions concerning traditions arise during holidays.

Late one November Lilly noticed that a woman attending her lecture seemed particularly preoccupied. At the conclusion of her talk, Lilly turned to her. "Any questions?" she asked. Softly, the woman began to speak of her problem.

In just a few weeks, she explained, she and her children would celebrate their first Christmas without a husband or father. They had been invited to her cousin's home, but there they would be surrounded by women with their husbands beside them and by children on their fathers' knees. She could, she quickly added, spare herself the anguish of this experience by remaining at home and attempting *to create Christmas for her children by herself. The woman paused and looked up at Lilly, begging for an answer.*

Lilly asked the woman to close her eyes for a moment and visualize her options, imagining how each might feel. The woman did this. First, she pictured the trip to her cousin's in Maine and the noisy, festive Christmas that awaited them there.

When she began to think about staying at home, her eyes opened after a few seconds. They were filled with tears. "I could not bear to stay home," she said suddenly. "And, while going to my cousin's will be difficult, and probably painful, it is the better decision for us. I have neither the heart nor the energy now to have Christmas on my own."

Holidays and special occasions often present an opportunity for reflection on the family's connection to the lost parent through a discussion of his values and ideals. Surviving mothers and fathers should always, through memories and anecdotes, keep alive the reality and humanity of the parent their children have lost. ("Do you remember how Daddy loved to sing Christmas carols but always forgot the words?") Its tempting to idealize a lost loved one, but doing so ultimately creates a hollow idol where a real human being once stood.

Grieving children need the space to move away from their families too. They need the support of their own special friends, who view them as the center of the tragedy rather than as a sidelined member of a collective despair. And, like adults, they need work and interests that will reconnect them to life.

School can help. An understanding teacher can support a bereaved child by providing a listening ear when one is needed and a sensitivity to the difficulties of concentration and adjustment. (Make sure principals and teachers know your child's background!) School is a place where your child can be just a kid for several hours a day, and this opportunity minimizes the burden of loss that awaits him or her at home.

Children also need the aunts, uncles, teachers, coaches, and family friends who can temporarily fill the many different roles left empty by a parent's death. Children need a few heroes and heroines who can inspire dreams to grow again.

Abby's family spent two weeks of every summer in the Adirondacks, and the streams and lakes of those mountains became her hallowed waters. On a sandy cove of Lake Paradox, her passion for fishing was born. Abby watched in wonder as fishermen set out at dusk on the lake's still waters. She longed for a pole and a box of lures. Yet as she dreamed, she realized sadly that, even if she had them, she wouldn't know what to do with them. Her mother was indifferent to leaping bass and squeamish about handling worms.

Then Abby struck up a friendship with Mr. Giese, a resident of a neighboring cabin and an avid fisherman. Mr. Giese was delighted by Abby's enthusiasm for his cherished pastime. He took her fishing. He taught her how to bait her hook; he showed her how to cast.

Abby has her own rod and tackle box now, and she's saving toward a minnow trap. Her family has moved to an area where streams and fishing ponds abound. But she still eagerly awaits the annual fishing trip with Mr. Giese, who each year rekindles her dream of catching the big one.

By sharing his enthusiasm, Mr. Giese eased the ache in one child's heart. And while one person alone can never fill the void a parent's death has left, he or she can help by replacing emptiness with warmth, affection, and the sharing of simple pleasures. Surrogates like these, when they are very well known and trusted, should be encouraged. The child's natural instinct for small adventures should be fostered too.

A child experiences the world more immediately and intensely than does an adult, who has learned to filter experience through the intellect. You who grieve while you struggle to raise your children alone may find that it is through your offspring that your own eyes are opened. If you can still your grief long enough to admire a marble in your son's hand or a fading flower in your daughter's, you can, even while sorrowing, share the joys of the earth with your children.

POINTS TO REMEMBER

1. Children mourn erratically, alternating days of despair with days of absorption in life.

2. If you are the parent of a bereaved child, don't be alarmed by this seeming inconstancy. Don't pressure your child into cheerfulness or sorrow.

3. Watch carefully for the warning signs that indicate your child has assumed responsibility for his lost parent's death. If you cannot relieve your child of this burden of guilt, seek professional help immediately.

4. As your children grow, understand that they must re-evaluate the meaning of their loss at each new stage of development, integrating the values of the lost parent with the rest of their lives.

5. Realize that the way in which your child initially responds to death will depend on his age and development at the time of loss as well as other factors.

6. Don't be too alarmed if your children seem to deny their loss when confronted by the difference it creates between them and their friends. (Many grown-ups aren't too thrilled about being "different" either.)

7. On the other hand, don't be too shocked if you have a child who attempts to use that difference for gain. (A few adults have been known to do this too.)

8. After a death all children become concerned about their own safety: the younger the child, the greater the concern.

9. Fears relating to personal safety are heightened by the worry that the remaining parent may abandon them.

10. A child may feel threatened or rejected by her parent's grief.

11. Adolescents on the brink of assuming full responsibility for their lives may reject any parental grief that hints that adulthood is not all it's cracked up to be.

12. Recognize that the charge "I wish you had died instead" is often a plea for the return of order and stability. Most children feel this way at some point in the grieving process.

13. When comforting your children, beware of the pitfall of undisciplined compassion. Overcompensation for a child's loss may create a little monster.

14. Remember that as a parent you have the wisdom and life experience that must determine how the monies of your household are dispensed.

15. Allow your children to participate in the reallocation of the chores that keep a household running.

16. Give your children a voice in the new family traditions that must be formed when a death disrupts the old ones.

17. Carefully review your plans and options for holidays and special family occasions. Don't attempt more than you can handle.

18. Keep the reality and humanity of the lost parent alive for your children by telling and retelling the stories of his or her life.

19. Let your children move away from the family circle a bit toward the friends and surrogates who can help to fill death's void.

20. Stop a moment to view the world through the eyes of your child; reawaken to its wonders.

7 | Grief's Long Arm: The Readjustment of the Extended Family and Friends

And can it be that in a world so full and busy, the loss of one weak creature makes a void in any heart, so wide and deep that nothing but the width and depth of vast eternity can fill it up!
—CHARLES DICKENS, DOMBEY AND SON

When a human being dies, the grief that death evokes spins out in ever-widening circles like the concentric rings made by a stone tossed into a pond. As the mourners gather and the letters of condolence pile up on the desk, it seems astonishing that one life could have touched so many so deeply. To be sure, there are acquaintances who, because they knew her only superficially, are merely observing formalities. There may be others who, having viewed his life as a stepping-stone for some personal gain, select a drug-store card and then turn again to their own pursuits. But there are far more who, attending the funeral or writing from their hearts, will be profoundly altered by this death. Those who knew him long will long miss him. Those who knew her intimately will mourn deeply. Those who loved him most will despair.

In the center of this circle, along with the surviving spouse and the dependent children, are the adult children and parents of the deceased.

When adult children lose a parent, the difference between their grief and that of their youthful counterparts is based on their years of life experience and the maturity that experience has granted. Children who are beyond adolescence have already suffered some degree of loss in their lives. If healthy, they have separated from their parents and forged important relationships. And, unlike the very young child, they have learned that people who separate can also meet again. They have learned to care for themselves and, in the best of situations, to accept the responsibilities of their dreams and goals. They are adults now, and they grieve like adults. The loss of a parent provokes all the painful feelings of grief, along with the fear that this irretrievable loss will change the way they see themselves and their world. They feel older. An essential part of their history has ended, and sobered by the sudden push toward a more mature generation, they grieve for both the lost parent and themselves.

The younger the adult, the more apt he is to feel deprived. No sooner has he moved away from home than its security shatters behind him. Not only does the door of his childhood bang closed but the doors to the future he expected slam shut as well. That comforting known—to which he felt he could, when needy, return—exists no longer. Gone too is the anticipation of the still-to-come triumphs that would have doubled in value when shared with that parent. Adult children who have not yet started families of their own may feel that they've been set adrift.

A year after her father's death, twenty-five-year-old Julie wept when her mother returned from her first long-distance journey on her own. "I'm so glad to see you," Julie repeated over and over again. "Now that you're home, I'm not an orphan any more."

In contrast, adults in their thirties and forties—caught up in their own jobs, families, and homes—are both aided and frustrated by the everyday demands that prevent them from fully expressing their grief.

"When Mother died, I kept wishing that mourning dress had not gone out of fashion," said Mary. "Unable to ignore my responsibilities, I needed some way to say to the world: 'This is what has happened to me. This is the most important issue in my life right now.'"

Middle-aged, heavily burdened adults have a complex mourning process. These adult children mourn not only for the missing parent, but for time unshared, words unspoken, and a relationship that might have been fuller if only they had not been so busy. Sometimes these guilty feelings can provoke angry recriminations at the surviving parent.

The balance of power between parents and their children is frequently upset when one parent dies, and the way this balance is restored is critical to the family's ability to function. At the time of the death, however, this power is apt to fall on the executor of the will. The executor, appointed by the deceased, is most often either the remaining parent or an adult child. If the relationship between that parent and his or her children is unstable, a great deal of unhappiness can be stirred up over the issues under the control of the will. (Sadly, the amount of the inheritance often corresponds to the degree of resulting unhappiness.) The child who has turned in financial need to the generosity of the deceased parent may find himself on shifting sands when the other parent inherits the purse strings. But it is apt to be even harder for the parent who, with all his or her faculties intact, must now seek approval from his or her child for expenditures. It will take sensitivity and understanding on the parts of both parent and child before these new roles can be accepted.

There are likely to be other tough challenges for the grown-up child, and the family balance may tip once more when a capable, decision-making child steps out in front of his or her siblings, accepting the brunt of these responsibilities. If the surviving parent is disabled, in poor health, or simply unable to cope with the difficulties of living alone, the encouragement of his children may enable him to make the changes that would better the quality of his existence. If, on the other hand, he is comfortable and likes it "just fine where I am, thank you," then the support and approval of his children may provide the encouragement needed for him to learn to live successfully on his own.

A pattern of decision making that enables a surviving spouse to increase autonomy will invariably be better than one that doesn't. The relationship between the adult child and his or her parent should be just that: adult to adult. And while a child may greatly help a parent to make the first frightening decisions, ultimately both will be better served if the child becomes a resource rather than a refuge. When this goal has been achieved, all family members are freed to respect one another as equals.

Parents who lose an adult child are confronted by different problems. They feel deprived of not only the son or daughter they raised but of their own posterity embodied in this child as well.

When we are young, for a short time we are joyfully unaware of the knowledge that our lives—and all others—will end. Then the cat gets hit by a car, or the little boy down the street loses his grandmother, and we receive an intimation of mortality. Forever after, the truths come hard and fast, and we learn to face the incredible prospect of losing our grandparents, our parents, and finally our own lives. However, we do not usually expect to face the loss of a child.

There are many ways in which surviving spouses can both help and be helped by their grieving parents-in-law. By understanding the nature of their loss, the widow or widower can encourage these stricken parents to transfer their hopes for immortality to their grandchildren. And because the grandchildren are so often in need of the special brand of nonjudgmental love and guidance that grandparents can pro-

vide, the potential for mutual support between these generations is infinite.

Unfortunately, this support sometimes breaks down
before it is given a chance to grow. During her years of coun-
seling, Lilly has discovered a problem that may develop,
depending on the sex of the surviving spouse.

When men with young children lose their wives, the
mother-in-law is apt to become a strong, helpful force in the
family's ongoing ability to function. She may even move in
for a while, mothering her daughter's children while she
teaches her son-in-law the skills he will need to raise his offspring alone. Later, when help is no longer needed, she is
likely to stay in close touch with the family, providing her
son-in-law and grandchildren with support and love and the
heritage that belonged to their mother.

However, when a woman with small children loses her
husband, the situation is often quite different. In this case, the
mother-in-law's mothering skills are not needed and if
offered are in danger of being misconstrued as interference.
Furthermore, a mother-in-law, desperate to share her grief
over the loss of her son with someone who can understand,
may turn to her daughter-in-law with the expectation of
deepening their bond through the sharing of their sorrow.
But the widow, who is struggling to assume leadership of her
family, may not be able at this point to give her sorrow the
upper hand. When the mother's need to express her grief
clashes with the wife's need to maintain control, a rift may
occur. If, however, the mother-in-law can discover other
avenues through which to support her son's family, the
extended family unit, though changed, will remain intact.

The sisters and brothers of the deceased are very much in
need of support and sympathy too, for this loss hits hard with
implications of their own mortality. They are also deprived
of their youth's constant companion and of one of the few (if
not the only) sharers of the present who truly understood
their past. Tormented by a "There but for the grace of God
go I" response, siblings may feel compelled to reevaluate

their lives and priorities. If their grief can be recognized and their resources directed toward the remaining spouse and their nieces and nephews, new relationships and understandings can be formed.

Felicia, who had never married, was happily pursuing a career that promised tremendous power and recognition when her younger brother contracted a terminal disease and died. Suddenly she discovered that her job meant a lot less to her than she had thought it did. Although she remained interested in her work, she began to participate actively in caring for her brother's two small children while forging a mutually supportive relationship with his wife. Today Felicia feels that her life has been enhanced by these relationships.

While the loss of an individual can be expected to evoke anguish in the hearts of his immediate family's members, the depth of grief the surviving spouse's family can experience should never be underestimated either. Parents–in–law are often traumatized far beyond the extent that might be expected by the loss of the individual to whom they gave their child in marriage. The pretty girl who enticed their son from home or the young suitor who wooed away their daughter usually has become over the years a loved and trusted family member.

Margaret's father was profoundly changed by Marv's untimely death. The guiding force behind a large network of family, friends, and fellow professionals, he had started to relinquish some of what he considered his fatherly responsibilities to Marv, whom he had learned to trust with his most valued descendants. He had recently begun to travel, knowing he need not worry because Marv would be there, as he had been, for everyone in the family. His world was torn apart when Marv was killed, and he still feels the impact of Marv's loss.

He has found it difficult to be both a father to Margaret and a grandfather to her children. If when he is visiting Margaret's family a grandchild behaves unreasonably, Margaret's dad feels caught between these dual roles. Should he assume the benign expression of the nonjudgmental granddad, or would it be better to take on the sterner countenance of Margaret's father?

The parents-in-law may even feel that the surviving spouse begrudges them the years that have been denied to his or her mate.

The children-in-law of the deceased mourn too, both for the parent of their spouse and for their own children's lost heritage.

Lilly's daughter-in-law, Shelley, sat quietly in the living room amid the circle of mourners. She tried to get used to the idea that Ernest, her father-in-law, was gone. Five hours had passed since his death, and now, in the middle of the night, tears had been replaced by the quiet murmurs of memories and love. All of a sudden, Shelley burst into uncontrollable tears.

When she was able to speak, she explained that she had been overcome by the reality that Ernest would be forever unavailable not only to those in the room but to those as yet unborn. Shelley grieved for the grandfather her children would never know. (Four years later, a son was born to Shelley and her husband, David. Still in the delivery room, David looked at the infant son and became poignantly aware of the succession of generations. This was Ernest's grandson, and he decided to name the baby after his father.)

During the difficult months following a death, sisters, brothers, aunts, uncles, and cousins of the surviving spouse can be of great help to the bereaved family if there are strong bonds between them. These relatives can play useful roles in the survivor's future if they are willing to search inwardly for the ways they are best suited to aid and encourage.

The death of Karen's husband, Bill, seemed to create an unbridgeable distance between Karen and her younger sister, Colleen. In her late twenties, Colleen wanted to devote at least two more years to her career before she considered marriage. To imagine what the death of a not-yet-existent husband might feel like was totally beyond her powers of invention. Although Karen and Colleen had always been close, Karen's loss made Colleen (who needed to think of marriage in terms of its joys rather than its sorrows) uncomfortable.

Colleen's reticence hurt Karen's feelings, and after several awkward attempts Karen was forced to realize that visits helped neither of them. As the months passed, even their phone calls became less and less frequent.

About a year after Bill's death, Karen began to think seriously about looking for a job. The prospect terrified her. The night before her first interview, she laid out one outfit after another until the sight of her closet made her dizzy. She went to bed and then got up again. She went to the kitchen for milk and cookies, and, leaving the milk carton on the countertop, she carefully placed the cookie jar in the refrigerator. Then, suddenly remembering how she and Colleen had talked all through the night on the eve of her departure for college, she ran to the phone.

Colleen was delighted to hear from her. Here, at last, was an issue to which she could relate! Colleen reminded Karen that blue had always been her color, and Karen, laughing with relief, decided to wear her blue wool suit. Colleen then regaled Karen with accounts of the mishaps of her own job interviews, and the sisters talked far into the night.

Years have passed now, but Colleen has remained one of Karen's staunchest supporters, through not only her first interview but her first job, her first car, and her first date. Today, the bond these women despaired of losing is stronger than ever.

Relationships in mourning are especially complicated if the individual who died—and perhaps the surviving spouse as well—had families through former marriages. Blended families are under tremendous pressure when a parent (who is also a stepparent, a second spouse, and an ex-spouse) dies. There may be valuable possessions, bank accounts, and jointly owned properties to divide. Objects of sentimental value to one or both families that have not been willed to a specific individual must be assigned, and in the process people who never liked each other very much must work together at a time when everyone is in emotional turmoil. Hostilities long since buried may reawaken. The surviving spouse, who has barely the strength and will to manage his own family, must now confront the "ex." Even the most successfully blended families are apt to unravel when caught between the pulls of past and present loves.

Gregory brought a young son and daughter into his second marriage, and his wife, Deborah, brought three young boys. Although the children visited their respective former families regularly, for ten years this new family lived together and functioned well as a unit. Gregory made no distinction between his own children and his stepsons. When a child had trouble in school, needed a baseball coach, or wanted to learn to drive, he was there.

Nonetheless, soon after Deborah died it became clear that her children were the more profoundly affected. Gregory watched helplessly as little by little Deborah's sons turned in grief to their biological father. In time the other house, once the place for alternate weekends and school vacations, became their home. Slowly and painfully, the blended family vanished.

Along with family members who are in and out of the house during the weeks following the funeral are friends of the deceased. Friends too—although last on our long list of mourners—are powerfully affected by the loss of a cherished companion. That casually uttered phrase "You look like you've lost your best friend" is an observation based on solid insight.

A friendship is a chosen relationship rather than an inherited one. It grows through the bonds of experiences shared. Neither the elusive spark that ignited it nor the mutual participation in its growth can be replaced. A friend is lost, and that particular friendship can never be duplicated. This is a threatening loss and one that may instill guilt in those still living. "Why was he taken and why do I remain?" "What must I do now to feel worthy of my life?" If a friendship was doubled by the enjoyment two couples shared, the impact of the loss is increased.

For the elderly person the loss of a friend is especially difficult, for with each loss a piece of the past is chipped away. Soon there will be none left to remember the way things used to be, none to share the memories. These survivors must learn, through the years and the losses, how to maintain an unflagging optimism about the future and their place in it.

An elderly violinist whom Susan once interviewed had lost not only his wife but most of his friends as well. For two hours he held Susan spellbound with the stories of his life. The conversation leapt from topic to topic: art, travel, astrology, politics. This ninety-three-year-old musician not only still practiced every day, but continued to nurture an avid curiosity.

As Susan was leaving, he asked a favor of her. "I gathered from our conversation," he began, "that you know something about astrology. Could you possibly cast my chart for the next ten years? I want to know what's going to happen next."

When a human being dies, most of the mourning friends and family members will interact, to some degree, with the immediate remaining family of survivors. Some will respond helpfully; others may hurt. Those who are personally threatened by the loss—those who need to dwell in the land of myth, where only the members of other families die—may abandon the bereaved family. Their remarks—"He just didn't take proper care of himself"; "She always struck me as someone who'd die young"; "She'll never make it without him"—would be better left unsaid. Some friends may lurk on the sidelines, waiting for the widower who, overnight, has been transformed into "an available man" or the widow who "must be sexually starved by now." When these masqueraders come calling, reread the Points to Remember at the end of Chapter 1, especially noting number 18: "Distinguish the individuals who are good supporters from those who are not."

About six months after Joe's death, a too-suave and too-solicitous acquaintance put his arm around Susan's shoulders, looked deep into her eyes and whispered, "How are you doing sexually?"

"Fine," she replied, "but I'm having a lot of trouble with my driveway."

To this day, Susan regards this exchange as one of her most satisfying memories.

Some so-called friends may vanish at the first sign of sorrow, only to reappear several years later when the crisis has passed. At that point, the choice of whether or not to continue the friendship will be yours. You may find that, in spite of his desertion, this person is still fun to be with; on the other hand, you may feel you've outgrown this sometime friend.

Those who remain to help, adjusting their roles to the needs of the moment, will become stronger friends. And if you can acknowledge the very real grief that your supporters are experiencing, you will ease their sorrow by allowing it expression. Shared sorrows lose some of their sting, just as shared joys double in pleasure. All who mourn this death will find that a loss survived together is far less painful than a tragedy borne alone.

Margaret, during the writing of this chapter, became quite over-come as she reflected on those who when she despaired stayed by her side with open arms and hearts. Through the years she has remem-bered with special tenderness the friends who arrived with arms full of chrysanthemums, which they placed on the casket at the close of the funeral. She appreciates those family members and friends who will preface a decision with the words "Now, what would Marv have done?" Her love has grown for her neighbors who have always been there—good days and bad—for her and her family.

These are the mourners who choose to deal with grief by making life more bearable for the living. These are the family members and friends who, because death has touched them, have learned to revalue their relationships.

POINTS TO REMEMBER

1. Death affects many individuals beyond the circle of the immediate family.

2. Adult children mourn not only a lost parent, but a lost childhood, as well.

3. The younger the adult, the more the loss of a parent is apt to make him feel deprived of guidance and emotional support.

4. Middle-aged adults who lose a parent may feel guilty about the irretrievable time that was too crowded with responsibilities to be spent with an aging mother or father.

5. The balance of power between adult family members

may be upset by the conditions of the will, or by the person who takes charge of the problems created by the death.

6. Adult children can aid their surviving parent through the mourning process by encouraging a pattern of decision making, enabling the parent to increase his autonomy.

7. Parents whose adult child dies grieve for the loss of that child and for the posterity he represented.

8. The surviving spouse can help his parents-in-law through the loss of their child by encouraging them to transfer their hopes to their grandchildren.

9. When the surviving spouse is a male with dependent children, his mother-in-law can often teach him the skills he needs to raise a family on his own.

10. When a woman with small children loses her husband and the nurturing skills of her mother-in-law are not required, a distance may grow between them unless other areas of mutual support are cultivated.

11. Brothers and sisters of the deceased will find comfort in continuing or developing a meaningful relationship with the surviving spouse and family.

12. Parents of a surviving spouse often grieve deeply over the loss of a daughter-in-law or son-in-law and are apt to be confused about their responsibilities to their child and grandchildren.

13. Other relatives of the surviving spouse can help him by developing their own special areas of support and encouragement.

14. The loss of an individual may instill guilt in the minds of surviving friends, simply because they go on living.

15. For an elderly person, the loss of a friend is especially difficult because so much of the past disappears with that friend, and because the older one gets, the fewer old friends are left.

16. Elderly people can become survivors if they cultivate new interests—in hobbies, travel, relatives, and current events.

17. Not all friends will be supportive through a crisis of death. One loses one's spouse, and usually a few friends, too.
18. The surviving spouse can help friends and family through grief by recognizing their very real pain.
19. A loss survived in the company of family and friends is less painful than one borne alone.
20. A person's death makes those who loved him place new value on meaningful relationships.

8 | A Silver Thread of Hope: The Readjustment of the Spouse

Life seems more sweet that thou didst live,
And men more true that thou wert one;
Nothing is lost that thou didst give,
Nothing destroyed that thou hast done.
—ANNE BRONTË

*A*s the months lumbered by, Margaret began to notice that the stretches between depressions had grown longer. As she paused one day to reflect on this development, she realized that, as difficult as the days of depression might be, they were usually followed by a breakthrough in her understanding of her situation. In fact, depression often seemed to vanish at the precise moment she decided to confront any of the hard-to-face issues that stood between her and the life of her own she longed to discover.

The more she thought about it, the more certain she became that her cycles of depression and her new insights were connected; as deep as the pit she fell into could be, it was usually followed by a new perception of who she wanted to be and how to become that person. The realization filled her with hope. Margaret decided that during future days of despair she would tightly grasp this silver thread of hope and not let go until the next perception revealed itself.

During the passage of grief, a turning point is reached. It would be nice if this moment was accompanied by fireworks or a hallelujah chorus. More likely, though, it will pass unnoticed, or even be dismissed.

You may discover a new insight. You may dimly notice that you are feeling better, but you will probably feel that you are deluded. In fact, it may take several days or even weeks of feeling better before you dare to believe that something valid is happening. In the years to come, the story would be better if you could point back to one dramatic hour and say, "Here is where it happened. On this moment of this day, I began to change."

You have been changing all along, but it has taken you this long to see it. One day, after months of hopelessness, you will look back. You, like Margaret, will see growth, and hope will fill your heart.

This is not the despairing hope for the miracle that will bring your spouse back, nor is it the hard, bitter hope that prays for resignation to your loss. This is the firmer, surer hope for understanding and for the abilities (which you are beginning to believe you may have after all) that will help you not merely survive your loss but accept and eventually overcome it.

Exactly when in your mourning this turning point will occur none can predict. But for all mourners there can be a day, unique to each, when hope begins.

For some, this turning point takes longer to reach than for others. Although all mourners have at times experienced ambivalent feelings toward their mates, those who lived in difficult marriages with intensified ambivalence have more to resolve.

Elizabeth's marriage began with high hopes for a future of happiness with her husband, Tom. It turned into an endless battle with Tom's alcoholism. Elizabeth attended Al-Anon meetings and rejoiced when Tom joined AA. When he gave up, she despaired. Again and again Tom tried and Elizabeth supported. Each time he failed.

When a doctor informed Tom that if he didn't stop drinking it would soon kill him, Tom withdrew all his savings from the bank, cashed in his life insurance policy, and went to Europe, where he died of a heart attack. Elizabeth was left with a formal telegram from a foreign official, no money to support her three teenagers who had hoped to attend college, and the crushing weight of her unanswered questions.

Had she wasted all those years of her life? Should she have walked out on the marriage without trying to help? Should she have helped just once and then walked out? Could she have done more to help? Finally, she asked herself (since she could no longer ask Tom), how could he have left her in this impossible position? Then, ashamed of her anger, Elizabeth wondered what kind of person she could be to feel such fury toward someone who not only was dead but had lived his life in the grip of an incapacitating addiction.

Hidden beneath Elizabeth's anger, however, lay heartbreak and longing for the love on which her union with Tom had been founded. Without the hoped-for years of happiness to look back on, Elizabeth found herself caught in what seemed to be an endless cycle of anger and depression.

The attitudes of outsiders did nothing to speed Elizabeth's recovery of hope. Overheard phrases, such as "because she's better off without him" or "and what she saw in him I'll never know," did more than dismiss Tom; they belittled and undermined years of Elizabeth's life as well.

While anger and guilt are both normal reactions to death, feelings of extreme anger and guilt (which can complicate and lengthen the months of deepest grief) are apt to be most pronounced in those mourning suicides.

When her husband committed suicide, Cynthia soon discovered that any guilt she was not already experiencing would be provided by those around her. The first question everybody seemed to ask was some form of "Didn't he give you any warning?" In spite of the fact that Cynthia knew he had given no warning at all, the question finally drove her to a crisis intervention center.

Now, a year and a half later, Cynthia is still very angry. Her husband's death devastated not only her own life but the lives of her children as well. Cynthia today feels controlled, abandoned, betrayed, and unspeakably furious.

Even during the earliest days of their grief, both Elizabeth and Cynthia sensed that in order to embrace their futures they would first have to confront, and then accept, their pasts. To look forward, all who grieve must first look back. When the past has been painful, the battle for understanding, forgiveness, and acceptance will summon all the courage and compassion the desperate survivor possesses.

The inspiration needed for this confrontation can be found in the words of *De Profundis* by Oscar Wilde, who while in prison wrote, "During the last few months I have, after terrible difficulties and struggles, been able to comprehend some of the lessons hidden in the heart of pain. Clergymen and people who use phrases without wisdom sometimes talk of suffering as a mystery. It is really a revelation. One discerns things one never discerned before."

After one ghastly depression, Margaret took a long, hard look at the person she had been in her marriage. She saw that during the years of her life with Marv, she had unconsciously taken the role of the volatile mate, while Marv had shouldered the responsibilities of the thoughtful, steady partner. Margaret had admired Marv's steadiness; he had been drawn to her verve. Marv had seen to it that the soup was nutritious; Margaret had tossed in the spices and then stirred up the pot. The marriage had been neither too bland nor too spicy.

Margaret, who had retained this image of herself during the months that followed Marv's death, now felt crippled. She'd had the uneasy suspicion that you could not run a household and lead your children on the strength of verve alone. Although she managed to wear a confident face for the outside world, she knew its expression was forced. She envisioned the years to come fearfully, watching herself grow older without Marv. Then the revelation occurred.

Suddenly Margaret could see that her volatility, rather than being an integral part of her personality, was necessary at the time. She wasn't patient or methodical because those traits weren't required of her.

A great weight lifted. From that day on, Margaret began to search within herself for the patience and equanimity her new situation demanded. Much to her surprise, she found the insights that would transform her from half of a couple to a whole and balanced individual.

Here, at last, is where character enters the picture! Remember when character was so miserably lacking during the earlier days of grief? These are the hours during which it appears and will develop if you faithfully nourish its growth.

Now you begin to be conscious of active choice. To be sure, during the weeks and months that followed your loss, you survived. You dressed, ate, shopped, worked, cleaned, and coped with children. Perhaps you learned to live alone for the first time in your life. You learned about the domestic contributions of your partner, either by figuring out for yourself or by finding someone who could. But most of this you did instinctively, your actions governed by a self-protective intuition.

Now, at this turning point, you have the satisfaction of viewing how far you have come and the challenge of anticipating the growth and effort that will be needed in the days ahead. This review of who you are in the midst of your loss will provide you with an update of your mental map of the world and your place in it. It is a giant step that must be taken if, at the end of your journey, you are to reach the sense of wholeness on which the rest of your life can be built.

Take a careful look at the person you were in your marriage. Which characteristics did you not have then that you wish you had now? Have you changed in ways that can be seen already?

Mary Jo cleaned out her closet a few months after her husband's death. She was surprised to discover that half of her clothing (gifts from her mother) had lace collars and frills on the sleeves; the other

*half (gifts from her husband) consisted almost entirely of blue denim.
She was dismayed when she realized that she didn't own even one
piece of clothing that she particularly liked. In fact, she wasn't sure
what she did like.*

*Mary Jo had spent years dressing to please her husband (except
for the occasions when her mother came to visit). Now, feeling dangerously liberated, Mary Jo drove straight to Bloomingdale's and
bought the first dress that struck her fancy.*

When you are able to see your marital relationship in its
entirety and have embraced both its strengths and its weaknesses, you need to determine which parts of the relationship
remain relevant to your present existence. You need to know
which elements can be left behind and which can be retained
as you move forward. How do you reach these life-shaping
determinations?

Aiming high, try to form a mental image of the human
being you would like to be. The choices you make now will
help to create the person you become. Many of these choices
won't be easy; there is more at stake here than lacy collars and
denim jumpers.

As you struggle to acquire the traits that are demanded
by your present and those that will enlarge your future,
remember that suffering doesn't automatically give birth to
wisdom. (If it did, we'd live in a very wise world.) Wisdom is
not bestowed as some sort of bonus for surviving pain but
must be sought—and even fought for—from the very center
of that pain.

There will still be periods of deep grief and depression.
There may still be obstacles that block your insight or impede
your growth. And while much can be accomplished on your
own, if you find yourself repeatedly running into a mountain
of impediment, one of the first active choices you may wish
to make is to seek the professional help that will enable you to
scale its peak. You already have an inkling of the limitless
world that lies beyond.

*Eighty-year-old Walter was a diabetic whose wife, Emma,
cared for him well. Their house was in perfect condition; in the
garden flowers bloomed abundantly.*

When Emma died, Walter was left completely alone. It wasn't long before the shining woodwork faded and the gleaming silver tarnished. Weeds appeared where flowers had so recently bloomed. Walter couldn't keep up with it all.

Slowly he began to realize all Emma had done for him. Why had he not seen it before? She must have worked herself to death caring for me, thought Walter, overcome with remorse.

As the house continued to lose its luster, Walter's guilt grew. When it became so large and bullying that it elbowed all insight aside, Walter sought help. He went to Lilly; he confessed.

"What would Emma have said if you had offered her a maid and a gardener?" Lilly asked.

"She would have been horrified by the very idea," Walter quickly responded. "And she would have been furious with me for making the suggestion."

Lilly smiled. "Then you see," she explained softly, "the life she lived is the life she chose."

Tears of relief and gratitude sprang to Walter's eyes. He walked out of Lilly's office standing tall, awed by his sudden comprehension of the depth of Emma's love.

No, Walter didn't go home and live happily ever after. His guilt didn't vanish overnight. But he felt a lot better.

Walter was already wiser. He had learned what to do with guilt. And each time he spoke with Lilly, he grew more confident of his worth. After all, he figured, he must be pretty special to have been loved so much by a woman like Emma.

When Walter put guilt in its place, he was able to survey his situation more realistically. His energies were freed to determine the needs and desires of his new life.

What are the needs of *your* new life? Are they being met as well as they can be within the framework of your particular circumstances?

During the course of these chapters, you have been introduced to the concept Lilly calls Choosing Twenty People To Fill One Pair of Shoes. How have you succeeded in this regard? Have you found the professionals (accountants and lawyers) who can help you understand and control the legal and monetary complexities of your situation? Have you acquired the domestic help you need (housekeepers, baby-sitters, cleaning people, plumbers, caretakers, gardeners, leaf rakers, driveway shovelers) to keep your household running smoothly? Do you have a good car mechanic? Have you discovered those friends who can be counted on for sound, unbiased advice?

And what about the emotional areas of your life? Have you determined which friends are good listeners and which provide a ready source of comfort? Are there one or two stalwart souls who always manage to be there when you need them? Are there some who are eager to join you on a weekend for a movie or a round of Scrabble? Have you overlooked the importance of touch? Do you know some good huggers? Have you a friend who'll put a strong arm around your shoulders at those moments when courage falters? Are there some you know who quicken to the sharing of a dream? Are there others who relish the exchange of a day's more homely details?

If you have tapped the resources of both friends and family and still are left with crying needs unmet, have you considered a support group? Have you opened the doors that can lead to the formation of new friendships? Friends acquired since the death of your mate can provide a new perspective. They accept you as you are when they meet you, and, unlike old friends, do not see you as the surviving half of a relationship.

Of course, even if you are fortunate enough to have the support of all these professionals and friends at your fingertips, they will not replace your loss. But they will help to sustain you during the time it will take for you to assimilate the best of your marriage into the bedrock of your being. Often, too, loving friends and family members can supply the nourishment so necessary to the formation of the new dreams and goals that will soon shape your future.

During these months of dependence on those who choose to stand by you, you will probably feel uncomfortable as you continue to accept so much from so many while giving so little. Never mind. Give what you can, and accept the help you need gratefully. Remember that many who support you now are answering the demands of their own grief. Remember, too, that the appreciative and wholehearted acceptance of a gift is often a gift in itself. Besides, your day for giving will come. Just be sure to add the qualities of generosity and compassion to that image of the human being you hope to become.

Now, take a deep breath and look squarely at those problems that may have developed in some of your friendships since that first awful week of the funeral. What is happening with that group of special couples who for years formed the teams of the sports you played or sat beside you at concerts? Do they leave you, do you leave them, or do the dynamics of the relationships adjust to fit the new reality? Do your friends understand that the dinner invitations they extend are not likely to be reciprocated for a while? Have you learned to cope with being the only guest at the table without a husband or a wife? With certain people, do you feel less like a person and more like a reminder of grim mortality? Must you lose once-meaningful relationships?

All these problems can, and usually do, develop at this time. Some you can control; some you cannot. Look carefully at your relationships in the light of what you are able to bring to them and what you hope to receive from them. Try to determine which are most mutually supportive. Keep a wary eye open for those without the flexibility to adjust to the demands of the new situation. Try not to be hurt by the individuals who, afraid to stand so close to death, seem to back away just when you need them the most. Some relationships you will probably not be able to save.

Nevertheless, trying to keep the old, dear friends will be the happiest choice for most survivors. But to do this both sides of the friendship will have to compromise.

Harriet and her husband, Jerry, had been part of a lively set of couples who often met casually for dinner and bridge on Saturday nights. When Jerry died Harriet immediately and resolutely refused all luncheon invitations from the women of this group. She was not going to let widowhood demote her from Saturday evenings of dinner and games to Wednesday lunches crowded into the middle of some pitying woman's busy workday. Not on your life. For Harriet, it was going to be Saturday night dinners or nothing at all.

Occasionally the old set did include Harriet in their weekend fun. But because bridge is a game designed for four players (or eight or twelve, if the host has more than one table), it didn't take long before Harriet achieved that nothing-at-all status she herself had dictated.

So Harriet sat home alone, feeding her grief with anger and resentment toward the friends who had dropped her at the hour of her greatest need. Months passed before she was able to swallow her pride and issue her own luncheon invitations. A year went by before she found the courage to attempt a couples dinner. That was the year in which Harriet discovered the value of a variety of relationships.

Another relationship problem that descends upon many a surprised survivor is the seemingly contented friend's confession of his or her marital problems. The experience of surviving the death of your mate makes others view you as a person who has really been through something (and, heaven knows, that's true). In the eyes of outsiders, grief turns almost instantly into compassion and understanding. Friends tend to detect these virtues in you prematurely. Three weeks after the funeral, the phone may start ringing, the sad stories unfolding. If the caller belongs to the opposite sex, the scenario, unfortunately, is usually predictable, starting with problems in common and ending with even more problems in common.

During your months of mourning, a friend's unburdening of his or her most personal problems can greatly increase your own pain. And although you care deeply for the persons involved, it is usually wisest to excuse yourself from the direct line of another's sorrow or anger until you are strong enough to be of real help.

Within weeks of her husband's death, good friends coaxed Jill into the middle of their very ugly divorce. Nightly she listened to both sides ad nauseam. This problem was compounded by the fact that Jill had two phones and two phone numbers; far too often both parties were on the lines simultaneously. In a desperate attempt to be as wise and compassionate as her friends seemed to need her to be, Jill piled misery upon misery onto her own despair. Finally, numbed by her own pain, Jill was forced to acknowledge that she was unable to empathize with theirs. She gave up. The couple divorced. Neither party speaks to her today.

Remember that you are in a period of transition, working hard to discover your self and your direction, still in too much emotional pain to be able to deal with problematic or hurtful relationships. Romance, too, can be a dangerous proposition at this point. You would be wise to let all knights in shining armor (and their female equivalents) gallop right past your door; when viewed through tears, their dazzle can be blinding.

Evaluate the sincerity of those around you. Don't feel selfish about trying to determine what your friends and family can do to support you through this critical time. Don't feel shy about continuing to express your needs. Sometimes the simple expression of a need is all it takes to turn a floundering relationship into a fulfilling one. Learn from your mistakes, and don't hesitate to let your friends know which situations you can handle and which still give you trouble.

When Margaret's friends from Chapter 4 called a second time to invite her to dinner and the theater, she responded warmly to their invitation. "Dinner and a show sounds great! But, you know," she explained, "the last time I was with you I learned that I am still not strong enough to bear the drive on I-95 past the spot where Marv was killed."

"Don't give it another thought," her caller interrupted. "We like the backwoods route better anyway."

The friends who bear with you are the ones you will want to keep. You need those individuals who want to be in your life in a way that works for both of you. Furthermore, during this period of transition, your friends and family are still fulfilling aspects of the role your spouse once played. It is good for them and for you to understand and value that contribution.

As the dynamics of your relationships shift and settle

into the reality of the present, you may find that changes occur in the more private areas of your life as well. Without an evening's companion, you may be going to bed earlier, rising in time to catch the dawn. To avoid that awakening sensation of loss, you may one day abruptly decide to sleep on the other side of the bed, filling the emptiness with a pile of favorite books and perhaps the telephone too. You may decide to move the bed; or, if you suddenly feel the need for a whole new space you may claim the guest room for your own.

Now, when the mood for reorganization strikes, may be a good time to dispose of your mate's clothing. If you feel ready to tackle this very tough job but are afraid to start, try Lilly's strategy: pack up a carton of shoes and put it in the basement. If this feels okay, giving them away will be easier. As you become increasingly aware that the love and values of your marriage are within you, your spouse's clothing will become just clothing.

And what about your wedding ring? Do you wear it for the rest of your life? Do you put it safely away for your children to inherit? Like all private matters, this is a totally individual decision. Ernie has never removed his. Millie wears hers on a chain around her neck. Margaret moved hers to her other hand. Janet's resides in her blue velvet box of treasures. Do what feels right for you.

As you sense your life and your relationships changing, you may find comfort in completing some of the projects your spouse could not. You may wish to plant the garden you so often envisioned together. You may find satisfaction in contributing to that charity she championed. You may even want to roll up your sleeves and take over his business! The perpetuation of your partner's goals and ideals will help you to realize that change means not disloyalty but acceptance.

Do all you can to encourage acceptance. Welcome the mornings that you awaken looking forward to something. Rejoice at the return of anticipation and delight. Observe your growth by starting some long-term project by which your progress can be measured.

Susan decided to make a quilt for Dale, her piano teacher. Although not a seamstress, she decided to make it entirely by hand. She collected scraps of all the colors she could find and carefully began to stitch them together. She carried her quilt to waiting rooms, where she stitched through children's checkups, dental appointments, and flute lessons. She carried it to bed where, when the late show became too engrossing, she stitched it to her nightgown. On these nights she often gave up, throwing both the nightgown and the quilt into the closet.

But on the days when shattered confidence seemed to reduce her to nothingness, she went back to the closet and looked at the quilt again. Each time she went back, it had grown. I must be someone, she would think, because I have chosen all these colors and have pieced them all together. Then, extricating her nightgown, she would begin work on it once more.

It took her three years to finish the quilt, and when she was done she knew she had accomplished something. So she wrapped it up one morning, carried it to her piano lesson, and presented it to Dale. In return for the silver thread of hope that he had handed her each Thursday, she offered all the colors she had been able to find.

Try to find something you want to do, and run the risk of doing it. You may not want to try it again for a while, but the experience of trying once will increase your estimation of your courage and worth. And each time that estimation rises, you are one step closer to having the character and wisdom you envisioned not so long ago.

"In our present," Paul Tillich said, "our future and our past are ours." It is by accepting your past, and by uniting the values and ideals of your marriage with your present, that you can find your future. And when at last you step whole into that future, you will know that the best of your marriage is within you and will always be there when you need it.

POINTS TO REMEMBER

1. During the months of grief, each mourner can reach a turning point in his or her own way and time.

2. Stop. Look back at the growth you have achieved even in the midst of grief. Allow the knowledge of your progress to fill you with hope.

3. Understand that mourners, before moving forward into their futures, must first accept their pasts.

4. Mourners of difficult marriages will have more to resolve than those who grieve for happier unions.

5. Examine your depressions for the seeds of growth hiding within them. Are there problems you have been afraid to face?

6. Start to live with the consciousness of active choice. Understand that the choices you make now will shape the person you become.

7. Take a close look at the person you were within your marriage and try to determine which characteristics you now need that you did not have then.

8. Form a mental image of the human being you would like to become someday.

9. Surviving grief and acquiring wisdom are not synonymous; if you want wisdom, you're going to have to work for it.

10. If your insight into the patterns of your grief is blocked, seek professional help.

11. Ask yourself: What are my needs today, and how well are they being met?

12. Look carefully at any problems grief may have caused in your relationships.

13. Reevaluate your relationships, trying to determine which are most mutually supportive. Realize that you need those individuals who want to be in your life in a way that works for both of you.

14. If friendships are to survive the ordeal of loss, compromises on both sides will be required.

15. Be patient with yourself. Recognize that until you are stronger it will be difficult to carry a friend's problems on top of your own.

16. Assess the sincerity of those around you, and deal with your friends honestly; don't hesitate to let them know which situations you can handle and which you cannot.

17. Observe the changes occurring in your private life, and recognize that active choice is now operative in this area too.

18. Base personal choices on what feels right for you.

19. Do what you can to perpetuate your mate's ideals, and learn that change means not disloyalty but acceptance.

20. Try to find something you want to do, and run the risk of doing it.

Part III

IDENTITY
AND
FULFILLMENT

9 | In Pursuit of Your Dreams

Life shrinks or expands in proportion to one's courage.
—ANAÏS NIN, DIARIES

If one advances confidently in the direction of his dreams, and endeavors to live the life which he has imagined, he will meet with a success unexpected in common hours.
—HENRY DAVID THOREAU

Who are you now, and where are you going? Just what do you plan to do with your life? These are the tough questions that face all of us at cliff-hanging moments. Survivors, too, must reach the day when they begin the journey that will ultimately lead them to a world beyond grief. With the strengths of their marriage within them, they must step through its door in pursuit of their dreams. They will arrive at the threshold bearing in their collective pasts the devastating experiences of loss that will change and at the same time strengthen both the way they ask questions and the answers they begin to find.

Who are you now, and how have you arrived at a point that you, a supposedly mature adult, must ask such a question? How is it that when we lose our mates, we also seem to lose our very selves?

We learn about ourselves from both internal and external clues. Having lived for most of your adult life as part of a couple, you have learned much about who you are and are not from your partner's feedback. You saw yourself through his or her eyes.

When your spouse dies, you are faced not only with the loss of the person who shared your life, but also with the loss of the person who validated a crucial and extensive part of your identity. Just how much of your identity is tied up in your partner depends on your gender, age, and individual propensities, and on the degree of independence you achieved before you married.

During the years of her life with Marv, Margaret, who married young, eagerly risked a wide variety of challenges. She knew that even if she fell on her face before a crowd, Marv loved her. And if Marv (who Margaret thought could walk on water) loved her, then no matter how many falls she took, she was a success. It was as simple as that.

Margaret's risk-taking tendencies were curtailed by Marv's death. Without his feedback, without his love, any fall would become a failure. And before a crowd of onlookers (who might not love her at all) a fall could all too easily turn into a disgrace.

Margaret, who had never lived on her own, had to seek the person within her who was separate from their relationship. It was only by learning to do this that she could begin to find herself. It is this elusive selfhood that holds the personal power of development and growth and determines the dreams you wish to pursue.

Survivors who have been dependent on their mates for knowledge of themselves face not only grief but an identity crisis too. In many respects the identity crisis of loss is quite different from identity crises other adults face. This crisis is unwanted, unprovoked, and often unexpected. Furthermore, shock and grief make foresight difficult, so that any effort that might have been used to overcome the identity crisis must be spent instead in overcoming the initial shock of the loss.

The problems accompanying an identity crisis after a death will, of course, differ from individual to individual and situation to situation. Survivors with dependent children will be confronted by the exhausting demands of earning a living while single-handedly running a household. Retired survivors will be faced by emptiness and shattered plans for future shared time. Ill survivors, once cared for by their mates, must now depend on their children, friends, or strangers. Yet, despite the differences of character and situation, there is much these survivors hold in common.

When a person is suddenly left alone, when the emotional structure that for years supported him or her lies in pieces, the survivor faces what psychiatrist Viktor Frankl called the "existential vacuum." He feels empty. Life appears meaningless. Although the survivor has the resources to go on living, he can't figure out why he should. He regresses to his neurotic extremes, his lowest common denominator of functioning, and has to proceed slowly and painfully to a point at which he is able to begin the search for a meaning and purpose for his life. "Who am I now?" he cries at last. "How can I make the rest of my life significant? Does the world owe me something, or do I owe me something? Is the world responsible for me, or am I responsible for me? Do I have any choices?" If he asks the question "What is the worst that can happen to me now?" he may be surprised to hear a voice inside himself respond with conviction: "The worst has happened already."

It is after the acceptance of loss that you are free to direct your energies to the rest of your life. It is here that the conscious search for a distinct individuality of your own begins. But how do you go about achieving selfhood?

You start by considering your childhood. Who were you before you were "we"? Are there remnants of that child that were put aside during the years of your marriage, unneeded and therefore unused? Are there lost or half-forgotten strands of yourself that can be reclaimed for the creation of your new identity? What personality traits have remained constant over the years? Which interests have endured? What are your skills, your values?

If you are unsure, look closely at your actions; they often reflect your beliefs. Scrutinize the parts of your life that form the whole: your career and public commitments; your personal affiliations; your opportunities for personal growth. Can you see any parts you would like to change? Are there musty talents in your attic that you would dust off and use, if only you dared?

You may feel that you don't want to risk changing any more than you've had to already. But you *will* change. Something monumental has happened to you, and it will change you if you don't seize control and change yourself. Did you ever read *Great Expectations* by Charles Dickens? Do you remember Miss Havisham, who, when her beloved deserted her on their wedding day, retired to live in seclusion, forever controlled by her loss? This is not the direction you want to take.

Change will often mean moving out of your safe routines into new, uncharted territory. It is apt to present itself in the form of a challenge.

Two days after his retirement, Mike's wife, Linda, was killed by a speeding car that jumped a highway divider. Although deep in grief, he felt compelled to urge legislators to install the barriers that would have prevented an accident of this kind. Mike used his new free time to write letters to his congressman, give interviews to reporters, and appear on both radio and television in an effort to stop similar fatalities. Eventually he was appointed to a regional commission that succeeded in pressuring the state department of transportation to act. The barriers were installed.

Many survivors are challenged by their anger into a response that benefits their communities. Linda's needless death raised Mike's

*consciousness of his community's welfare, and this awareness con-
tributed to the formation of his new identity. When the new Mike
stepped forth to meet his future, he took with him a heightened
sensitivity to and involvement in the safety of his fellow human
beings.*

Each of you can think back to some challenge you had
never handled before and were sure you never could. But you
did it. And the success of that venture brought an unfamiliar
feeling of accomplishment. This feeling is the beginning of a
new phase of confidence and self–esteem that will eventually
stimulate your dormant abilities and strengths. It's not something that happens overnight; but if you persevere it will happen.

*Susan's challenge, not surprisingly, was a musical one. She
had taken piano lessons since the age of seven but forsook them when
she became an adult. For years she hardly missed them. Then one
morning during the last months of Joe's life, she awoke gripped with
the need to play the piano well again.*

*There was a piano in her living room. But her repertoire,
which had once consisted of Bach, Beethoven, Schubert, and Sho-
stakovich, had been reduced by years of motherhood to something her
children called "The Running Song." This was a revved-up version
of "Oh, Dem Golden Slippers," played at breakneck speed while
her daughters, squealing with delight, raced around the house. Suddenly it wasn't enough.*

*Terrified by a crumbling future and desperate to find something
of her own that would endure, Susan searched for a teacher and was
given Dale's number. She had taken five lessons with him when
Joe's cancer reached his brain. Four months later he was dead.*

*Grief-stricken and exhausted, Susan dragged through the long,
senseless hours. She was up to her ears in preschool children and
endless time.*

*Did she use this time productively? Did she ease her grief with
music? She did not. She spent at least three hours each morning
thinking of all the reasons why she couldn't practice. And each
Thursday she drove miserably to her piano lesson, unprepared and
unwilling to change. If "The Running Song" had been good enough
for Joe and the children, it was good enough for her too.*

Then one morning Dale, who for months hadn't flinched at the hardships of teaching a stone, said quietly, "If you could practice, it might help."

And because she was so grateful to him for caring, she decided to try just a bit, twenty minutes each morning. She put her big toe in the water. And what she got for it was just a bit of progress.

A few weeks later Dale suggested that she might like to work on Chopin's Polonaise in F-sharp minor. Susan stared at him dumbfounded. She owned a recording of this tremendous piece, and she knew it was not a work for the faint of heart.

Who does he think he's kidding? she thought, driving home. Somehow the F-sharp minor polonaise and twenty minutes each morning didn't add up. She started listing reasons why she couldn't work on it: her hands weren't big enough, there were too many notes, she had too many children.

Nevertheless, when she got home she tried it. And, although her hands weren't big enough and there were too many notes and too many children, she stayed with it. Almost a year later (a year in which her practicing time increased to a half hour a day, then an hour, then two and any spare time she could find), she walked into her lesson, sat down, and played it. She had taken a half-forgotten strand of her childhood and reclaimed it as her own. She was, at last, in hot pursuit of a dream.

There is nothing easy about building a new identity, just as there is nothing easy about any part of the readjustment process. You must learn to make decisions independently, structuring your future on your own dreams rather than the dreams of others. You must learn to do things on your own. You must establish your changing identity with old friends, and you must seek new friendships.

These goals are achieved little by little, decision by decision, one step at a time. In the process you will discover within yourself the person who is independent of past, present, and future relationships—the you who can spend time alone and feel good about it rather than feel lonely. You will discover the self who provides security regardless of the events that transpire around you. This is the identity that enables you not only to survive but to prevail.

Do not, in the effort to achieve this sense of selfhood, expect to find a tidy outline for the rest of your life. You know only too well that you are not in control of the rest of your life. You can, however, take control of your direction. You can set up the goals for this week, next month, maybe even next year. You can take responsibility for your health and safety. You can reassess your financial position, readjusting and reallocating your resources. You can review your job situation, and if you find it lacking, you can strive for changes that will better it.

When Elizabeth was handed the telegram notifying her of Tom's death, she was also handed the responsibility for three teenagers, one dog, an old car, a large house, a small shop, and a real estate office. She cleaned the house, supervised the kids, walked the dog, and washed the car. She sat in her shop and waited on customers, except for the times when she had customers for houses, and then she put a sign on her door saying, "Be back soon." There was so much to do that there was no satisfaction, and certainly no fun, in any of it.

It took years of learning just who she was and what she wanted before Elizabeth, exhausted, awoke one morning to the dog's cold-nosed urgings and said to herself, "There has to be a better way."

There was. Elizabeth sold the shop and began working for another realtor, thus creating the time and the peace of mind she needed for rediscovering life's simple pleasures. Each morning she walked her dog to the lake, where together they beheld the breaking day. She felt like a new woman, and she was.

The experience of loss may change the way you view your work. Remember that the demands of readjustment are many and taxing. Does your job hinder or help your growth and development? Should you consider a different area of work? Do the accomplished tasks of your day increase your sense of personal worth or merely add to that already considerable list of demands on your time?

As Margaret mourned, she discovered that teaching no longer met her needs in the way it had when Marv lived. His death, she realized, had propelled her into a world peopled entirely by children.

She began each day with the supervision of her own children. Then she drove to school, where all day she taught and supervised the children of others. At night she returned home to further supervision of her offspring. Margaret was in desperate need of the company of some bright and self-supervised adults.

After prolonged soul-searching, Margaret took a leave of absence from school and secured an administrative job at an outstanding university, a long commute away. While this position lacks teaching's rewards, her days are now balanced by the companionship of her adult co-workers. Furthermore, by finding this challenging position, Margaret gained self-esteem and broadened her vision of the future.

If you have been out of the job market for a while and have decided (for either personal or financial reasons) you want to find work, now is the time to begin your quest. But before you head for the want ads, take another good look at your interests. What have you always longed to be, and what effort would it take to become it? If you have no clear–cut goal in mind, make a list of jobs or careers that appeal to you. You might want to talk to a career counselor. Then take a look at the want ads. If you have a position in mind but lack the required experience, try to determine the steps you must take to gain that experience. Think courageously! You are more apt to be hampered by your vision than by your skills.

Susan's children grew. Years had passed since Joe's death, and now even the twins boarded the school bus each morning. Susan's savings had dwindled, she owed taxes on her home and property, and her car was falling apart. She would either have to sell her house and move to a less expensive area or go to work. But what could she do?

She sat down and tried to look at her abilities objectively. The longer she looked, the clearer it became; she had no skills at all. When she considered her fear of math and her horror of machinery, she doubted if she could even qualify for the position at the cash register of her local supermarket. To be sure, she could play the piano a bit, but who woud ever want to hire her on the strength of that nebulous attribute? In the ballroom of the marketplace she was, quite clearly, a Cinderella—and there was no fairy godmother in sight.

Susan decided to move. She put her home on the market. She gave Mulberry, the family goat, away. And, when an offer was made on the house, she began to pack her bags.

At the eleventh hour, an old friend stopped by and offered her a job with one of the several companies he headed. He was, among other things, a pianist and the publisher of two music magazines. While the position he offered was not a musical one, Susan knew that if she accepted it she would be working side by side with musicians. "I'll take it," she said quickly.

So she went to work. When a position with one of the magazines opened up, her boss offered her the job. She took it.

The next morning Susan set off for her new job as a music editor. Her pumpkin had turned into a coach.

The love of something—your work, your garden, a game of tennis, a clarinet—will help you back onto the road to loving your life. And a person filled with love of life soon attracts other life lovers.

You must start with a positive and realistic self-image. Nourish your talents and accept your limitations. Find an idea or purpose. The scope of your idea will depend on your situation and abilities. It can be as far-reaching as world peace or as cozy as an embroidered tablecloth for your niece. It is the pursuit of this dream, big or small, that will carry you back into life's mainstream.

When you feel independent and secure, you will find that you have also earned the choice of living with or without another person in a meaningful relationship. While you were busy pursuing an idea, desperate need turned into independent choice.

There are some survivors, of course, who don't wait for this transformation to occur. Among these are far too many who are unaware that the potential for realizing selfhood lies within. Knowing themselves only through the eyes of their departed mates, they search desperately for other eyes to assure them. Gregarious survivors, too, may resist loneliness by attempting to date long before the problems of mourning have been resolved. Others leap into water way over their heads for a variety of complex (and even farfetched) reasons.

Margaret decided to go out with a man because a friend told her that she was becoming far too preoccupied with the lives of her children. Furious with both her friend and herself, Margaret denied the accusation by allowing this friend to select and arrange her first blind date. (It seemed a logical thing to do at the time).

Her date arrived. Margaret was charming; her children were polite. All went well. Then this very pleasant doctor made the mistake of asking Margaret for a second date.

It was strange how quickly things changed. All of a sudden, her children responded rudely to his phone call; Margaret responded incoherently. The stress became unbearable as the date of the dinner dance approached.

On the morning of the date, Margaret experienced an anxiety attack so severe that, placing a call to her unsuspecting dinner partner, she had him paged at the hospital. By the time he got to the phone, Margaret was so distraught that she could hardly speak. "I can't go to the dance tonight," she gasped into the receiver. "It's too hot."

Did Margaret learn anything from this misadventure? Not at first. Humiliated, her pride wounded, she kept trying. Several similar experiences occurred before she was able to understand that it was simply too early for her and her children to accept even the potential of a relationship in her life.

Most premature relationships fail. The primary reason for their collapse is the difficulty encountered when survivors try to split themselves and their energies by attempting to care for one person while grieving for another.

Those who wait until they are surer of themselves may find that the first relationship they choose is a transitional one. A transitional relationship is not necessarily romantic, although it may be. It is formed when two individuals develop an emotional link that replicates some of the feelings and patterns of the lost relationship while remaining unthreatening. The threat is avoided by the presence of an obstacle to total commitment. As long as the obstacle remains in place, these individuals are free to enjoy each other's company without assuming the responsibilities and commitment a deeper relationship would entail.

Kendra met Ted at a board meeting a year and a half after her husband's death. Even from across the room, she noticed him at once. He was a large man, and somehow his presence alone made her feel protected. When, as he was leaving, he touched her hand in a gesture of good-bye, Kendra was moved; it hadn't occurred to her that there was anyone in the world who might want to touch her hand. She left the meeting, but she tucked away the memory of the warm feelings Ted's presence had evoked.

Six months later, when the board was about to convene again, Kendra dropped Ted a note saying she hoped to see him then. He attended the meeting.

Soon Ted and Kendra were speaking daily on the phone and, although Ted lived in another city a considerable distance away (hence, an obstacle), they managed to see each other once or twice a month. Even though their backgrounds were very different (another obstacle), Ted became the person Kendra most enjoyed exchanging the day's events with (something she had shared with her husband). It was soon apparent that their values differed in many respects (a third obstacle) and many of their interests were dissimilar (a fourth), but Kendra and Ted didn't see each other often enough for that to bother them.

Kendra enthusiastically awaited Ted's calls and visits, shared the experiences of her days with him, and enjoyed the presence of a male in her life. At the same time, she reserved for herself the space she needed to strengthen her developing sense of selfhood and to determine in greater detail her direction.

Paradoxically, survivors who were most dependent on their mates and who have consequently fought the hardest for independence may become the most fearful when faced with the prospect of loving again. Equating love with a surrender of selfhood, they stand paralyzed between their longing for closeness and their triumphant independence. For these survivors, too, a transitional relationship is a good place to start. (A transitional relationship can, of course, grow into something deeper, something more permanent. People do change—you are proof of that—and love, when it gains a foothold, has been known to overcome many obstacles.)

When you are entering any close relationship, transitional or otherwise, it is important that the person with whom you choose it perceives you realistically (flaws and all) and respects the development of your abilities and strengths. Remember that through the powers of your devotion you will again catch glimpses of yourself in another's eyes. If what you see there is a caring tolerance and a loving respect, your personal growth, both within and without the relationship, can be enhanced.

A relationship is not, of course, necessary. Remarriage guarantees neither happiness nor a meaningful existence. But remarriage based on honest love and firm respect can certainly add depth to your life. Be sure that if you choose to keep your hard-won independence, you do so by choice and not out of fear. If, however, a new relationship is one of your dreams, you must have the courage to learn to love again. Reentering the single world can be terrifying. By doing so you test the vulnerabilities of your new identity and the strengths of your recently acquired selfhood.

We all need companionship and intimacy to varying degrees. And we all need time alone for reflection and growth. If, as you grow, you can learn to enjoy both the times together and those alone, you will experience the freedom that comes from making the choices that are right for you.

The Chinese character for "crisis" is made up of two elements: the symbol for danger and the symbol for opportunity. You have weathered the crisis. You have survived a brutal loss. Now, by facing the dangers and embracing the opportunities, you can enlarge and improve upon what remains: yourself.

POINTS TO REMEMBER

1. The loss of your mate can provoke an identity crisis.

2. Before you can determine where you are going, you must determine who you are.

3. To learn who you are, start by looking back to the person you were before you married.

4. Consciously evaluate your values and your skills.

5. Look closely at the separate aspects of your life. What do your actions and affiliations tell you about yourself?

6. Decide which, if any, parts of your life you would like to change.

7. Remember that even if you do not consciously seek to change yourself, the experience of loss will change you.

8. Recognize that change often presents itself in the form of a challenge.

9. The successful meeting of a challenge heralds a new phase of confidence that will stimulate your dormant abilities and strengths.

10. The effort to make your own decisions and do things on your own will contribute to the formation of your new identity.

11. Establish your changing identity with old friends, and seek new friendships.

12. Take control of your direction. Set up goals for this week, next month.

13. Reevaluate your job situation, and if you find it lacking strive to make the changes that will improve it.

14. If you are seeking employment, make sure your interests and abilities are in keeping with the opportunities you hope to find.

15. Remember that your future is more apt to be hampered by your vision than by your skills.

16. Accept your limitations realistically while moving forward.

17. Believe in yourself and in your will and ability to make something of your life.

18. Realize that attempts at establishing an intimate relationship are apt to fail if the problems of your mourning have not been resolved.

19. If you desire a close relationship but feel afraid and insecure, begin with a friendship that won't pressure you for commitment.

20. A certain amount of fear is normal; it can also be energizing. However, don't let fear block the path to your dreams. Face the dangers of your new life squarely, and courageously welcome its opportunities.

10 | Stronger in the Broken Places

A time to weep, and a time to laugh;
A time to mourn, and a time to dance.
—ECCLESIASTES 3:1

"*B*ut, how," pleaded Catherine, "will I know when I am truly and reliably 'okay'?"

"You will know," Lilly explained, "when you are able to put your grief away for a while.

"A day will come," she counseled, "when you will realize that you have forgiven your spouse for dying and yourself for continuing to live without him. This realization will be accompanied by an inner sense of balance that will allow you to put aside those feelings of anguish that stood between you and yourself, between you and your future."

*An expression of alarm crossed Catherine's face. "But I don't
want to forget him!" she exclaimed.*

*Lilly reassured her: "Those feelings are, after all, retrievable;
they will always be there for you if you should need them again.*

*"But," she encouraged, "you will soon find that you need them
less and less. As the pieces of the past begin to form a picture, you
will learn that your spouse was neither a saint nor a devil. As the
inflated images of grief's sorrow and anger shrink back to a more
lifelike size, you will recognize him for what he was: a human
being, best honored by the memory of his humanity. You will
cherish the memory of this very real human being with whom you
shared part of your life, and as you do your own humanity will
reawaken."*

*"I never realized that anything could hurt like this," Christo-
pher, the group's newcomer, interrupted. "Will I really feel better
someday?"*

The answer, Christopher, is a resounding *yes*. For all
who try to comprehend the lessons of pain, there is a thread
of hope. You *will* feel better someday. Yes, you can do it!

Is there anything to be gained from all this suffering?
Can one really turn such a negative experience into something positive?

You can if that is what you choose to do. As long as you
can take life's hardships and bend them into constructive
growth, you will not be defeated. For each of you, there is a
way. But you, in your uniqueness, must find your own
way.

"Work with all your strength to make your life significant," states Lilly. "Live fully. Don't compound your loss by
refusing to grow," Margaret cautions. "Contribute something to the world," says Susan.

We, along with many of the widows and widowers
interviewed for this book, have stepped beyond the question
Does the world owe me something or do I owe me something? To that, we answered, "I owe myself a meaningful
life." Then, we moved on to the next question. What do I
owe the world? That is what we ask ourselves today.

Although our answers have led us in different directions, it is this common concern that unifies our actions.

That's easy for you to say, all readers may think. You are strong. You were born with gifts and abilities.

So were you, we reply. We, too, were once heartsick and broken by loss. If we could do it, so can you!

It is indeed a hazardous journey. All who undertake it must combat the tremendous temptations to allow their losses to control their lives, to marry precipitously before learning to live well alone, to depend on their children instead of assuming responsibility for themselves, to defend their vulnerability with cynicism, allowing bitterness to become a part of their identities.

But this is a book about people who have attempted more than mere survival. This is a book about those who have sought to prevail.

Frances, a woman in her fifties, had lost the use of her legs in a car accident twenty years before her husband died. She had depended on him for everything, and when he died she didn't know how she would function.

With the help of family, friends, and a community agency, Frances began to build into her life the mechanical aids that would enable her to live on her own. Her physical therapist taught her to use the equipment that would make her mobile. He helped her redesign her home, making it livable and manageable. Everything in her apartment was rearranged to work for her. Then she learned to drive a van equipped with a self-operating lift that descends to street level with Frances and her wheelchair on it.

Frances seized control of the quality of her existence. She refused to turn her face to the wall and let widowhood and handicaps become the definition of her life. Instead she reached out—and sure enough, the emotional, social, and community supports she needed were there for her. These supports allowed Frances to experience and explore her grief fully and eventually to ask herself some questions about her goals for the rest of her life.

Today she directs an office for the handicapped and holds an office in a social group for widows and widowers. She is a justifiably proud survivor. She is also stronger than she ever imagined she could be. Faced with the choice of growing stronger or acquiescing to a forever-dependent state, Frances chose to grow.

Few of us can boast accomplishments as mighty as Frances's. Our victories are modest; our risks, far less grave. And yet each of us in our struggle through grief has become heroic, if you will, in ways we neither wanted to be nor in our wildest dreams imagined we could be.

Those whom you have met in these pages are today at different points of the survivor's journey. Some have traveled far beyond loss into the new lives that they, by their growth, have created. Others bravely continue to seek their identities and fight for their dreams.

Bob, who in Chapter 4 was so quick at intellectually comprehending grief's stages, has continued his climb up the corporate ladder. But success, he has learned, isn't enough. His personal life remains unsatisfying. His children have grown up, and he misses them. He has not yet filled the empty center left when the years of being his ill wife's caretaker ended.

But Bob is looking. In fact, he is seriously considering taking a leave of absence from the position he worked many years to achieve. Bob feels he needs some time and space to reevaluate his goals for the future. He realizes that his wife's death triggered a somewhat delayed identity crisis. Today he reexamines his values and his lifestyle, seeking the growth that will determine his direction.

Some, as we have seen, have longer and more complex periods of mourning than others. But as these survivors staunchly face the difficult issues of their lives, the oppressive weights begin to lift, the sense of self grows surer, and a clear direction beckons. Often it is through our weaknesses that our strengths are born. Dissatisfaction, when examined, leads to change. Fear, when confronted, turns to courage. Despair, when acknowledged and comforted, steps aside one day for the return of hope. The process through grief is a gradual one—two steps forward, one step back—with no lion's roar or list of credits to mark its ending. Most griefs fade rather than vanish, as growth replaces anguish.

There are exceptions to just about everything, however. Elizabeth is one of them.

One night, after seven long years of uphill, angry grief, Elizabeth went to bed. It was the week of the anniversary of Tom's death, and she had just arranged (for the seventh time) to have flowers in his name placed on the altar for the upcoming Sunday's church service. Depressed by the prospect of sitting through the service staring at Tom's flowers, Elizabeth dropped off to sleep.

She awoke the next morning with a vivid dream still clear in her mind. She and Tom had been alone in a room, a table between them. On the table were some highly official looking documents. Tom signed them first. He handed them to Elizabeth. Scared but excited, Elizabeth put her name beneath Tom's. Their eyes met as they solemnly shook hands. Clutching the papers, Elizabeth hurriedly left the room. She closed the door behind her and stopped to examine the documents. Suddenly she realized what she had done. She had officially divorced him. It was over.

Elizabeth got out of bed filled with relief. Later that morning she called the church and canceled the flowers. The lady at the other end of the line gasped and spluttered. "Cancel them," Elizabeth repeated happily and hung up. What she and Tom had been unable to resolve together, Elizabeth had at last resolved alone.

Her anger and depression vanished that night. Her subconscious mind had asserted itself, making the decision her conscious mind had wavered about for years. The tormenting what ifs and should I haves had been banished. The doors to her future opened wide.

Most survivors step more gently into their futures. Most have happier memories to take with them. Walter, who was plagued by guilt in Chapter 8, is a case in point.

With Lilly's help, Walter learned to thumb his nose at guilt. The vacancy created by the departure of guilt was soon filled by warm and wonderful memories of his marriage. And once the memories had staked their claim, Walter's interests reappeared.

Today, at age eighty-four, Walter leads a vigorous life, doing all the things he's always wanted to do with the time his retirement provided. He has found the household help he needs. He has main-

tained his old friendships while allowing himself plenty of time to pursue new relationships.

He may, however, choose not to marry again. As far as he's concerned, when you've had the love of a woman like Emma, you've had it all.

Elizabeth and Walter are stronger, surer individuals for their decisions. By resolving the haunting difficulties of her marriage, Elizabeth freed herself from her fears about any new relationships. Walter, by seeking help when guilt took over, learned how to allow his past to enhance his present. Each day, as he reclaims his interests and his friendships, he celebrates the memories of the love of a lifetime.

Bob, Elizabeth, and Walter have learned to face the challenges grief placed before them. They have grown and stretched in ways that life's calmer, safer days never demanded. They are stronger human beings today for their experiences and their efforts.

In James Agee's novel *A Death in the Family,* these thoughts ran through Mary Follet's mind as she first confronted her widowhood: "She thought that she had never before had a chance to realize the strength that human beings have, to endure; she loved and revered all those who had ever suffered, even those who had failed to endure. . . . She thought that now for the first time she began to know herself, and she gained extraordinary hope in this beginning of knowledge."

Mary Follet seemed to know intuitively that the process of grief would lead her to the challenges of attaining selfhood. She and the many survivors who have gone before her (and those who will most surely follow) must, sooner or later, ask How will I change, and who will I become now that I, alone, must determine the direction of my life and the quality of my existence?

Some of the survivors who have shared their experiences here are today discovering their answers to that question. Carrie, who in Chapter 2 hung from the cliff of economic disaster, is one of them.

Because she denied her loss by avoiding responsibility for her family's financial welfare, Carrie, when we left her, had put her home on the market and was desperately seeking a job. The house sold. She bought a condominium and moved into it with her son. But the financial havoc that precipitated her move had taken an even greater toll; it had propelled Carrie into a tailspin of diminishing self-esteem.

She was therefore astonished when one of the companies who had interviewed her called to offer her a highly responsible position. Most people would have been overjoyed by this opportunity for success and financial security. Carrie was appalled. She was afraid that she would fail. She had, after all, managed to lead her family to the edge of bankruptcy; now she had visions of leading an entire company into disaster. In fact, if she hadn't needed the money so badly, she would have turned the offer down.

But Carrie didn't fail. She grew. Painfully conscious of her shortcomings, Carrie learned to be meticulously conscientious. She worked harder than she'd ever worked before. And, wonder of wonders, she was promoted (in spite of some reluctance on her part) to an even more responsible position.

Although success weighed heavily for a while, Carrie thrives on it today. She assumes her responsibilities proudly and knows that her ability to honor them is the secret behind her independence and her fulfillment.

Carrie grew because she had to. Although she couldn't see it during the earlier stages of her grief, it was her willingness to take responsibility for her child that saved her. In spite of the fact that on one very dark night she had actually envied the vagabond existence of a bag lady, it had been the mental image of a little bag child trailing behind her that had given her the courage to accept the job.

The ability to embrace an opportunity isn't easy when you lack self-confidence. But how can you feel confident before you know yourself? Self and confidence meet only when that long, scary journey from despair to effort and from effort to accomplishment has been risked.

When Susan went to work, she had little faith in her skills.

Yet, unlike Carrie, she was able to accept the offer of a job without hesitation. Through diligent practicing, Susan had learned to trust her ability to try. She walked into the office that first terrifying morning determined to do her best.

The skills she acquired at work increased her confidence, and her growing sense of selfhood eventually enabled her to face her economic situation realistically. As her first daughter prepared to enter college, Susan finally accepted the fact that, even with a job, she was living in an area that cost more than she could afford.

She packed up her family and her bags; then she and her daughters said good-bye to their friends and, with tears streaming down their faces, departed. Susan had found the confidence she needed to create a new way of life for herself and her family. Today, she makes her contribution to the world by teaching piano lessons.

One of the strengths to be gained from hard times is learning to prepare for difficulties. Margaret, who in Chapter 4 learned much from her first dismal wedding anniversary alone, can now recognize a potentially depressing day far in advance and prepare for it.

This year Margaret's youngest child, Laura (who answered the door that day the policeman arrived and changed their world), will graduate from high school. Margaret's children have grown up.

The day of any parent's last child's leave-taking is often one of mixed emotions. While a child's departure to the adult world is usually a hopeful, exciting event, it can precipitate a spell of loneliness for those she leaves behind.

Loneliness, however, is not what Margaret has in mind. And she has been doing something to avoid it. Margaret spent the better part of the year in search of the challenging job she eventually secured. It is not by chance that she broadened her horizons, made new friends, and learned how to date. Margaret is not about to give loneliness the upper hand. She has seized control and is living fully.

Grief has taught us much. It has shrieked at us about our weaknesses. It has goaded us into our strengths. It has forced us to reexamine our goals and values. It has deprived us of the loving eyes that validated our identities and challenged us to find ourselves. Then it has dared us to search for the dream that will take us beyond its reach.

For Lilly, that journey through grief became the dream.

If, on the night Ernest died, someone had told Lilly that her anguish would lead her to helping others through grief, she would have been astounded. She would have traded any future for just one day of having Ernest by her side again. Lilly, like the rest of us, despaired. And then she grew.

She asked herself some hard questions. She completed several degrees. She searched for direction, and she looked for a job.

Then, in a most serendipitous way, she stumbled on an opportunity in which both her education and her personal experience of grief could be put to good use. "It was," she recalls with a smile, "the only situation in which being a widow was ever an advantage."

Today, Lilly's life is devoted to helping others through loss and beyond. Where she finds despair, she offers hope. What was once her anguish has become her calling. Those she has guided toward their futures can testify that hers is indeed a significant life.

But Lilly is not invincible—nor is Margaret, or Susan, or any of the others whose stories have been told in these pages. We worry about our finances, become exasperated with our children, and stumble as we strive to be worthy of the relationships we form.

But our journeys through grief have changed us. We are not as afraid of death as we used to be. We have learned that if something is not life threatening, it is manageable. We have learned that life is fragile and precious, and because of this realization we pursue our dreams and cherish our relationships with greater urgency. We know that the journey through grief can lead to the celebration of life, and we have learned that every human being has the choice to live life caringly or carelessly, with compassion or with bitterness, courageously or fearfully. We search each day for the caring, compassionate, courageous path. You, too, can make that choice.

For us, this book is ending. For those of you who have read it in grief, there may be chapters of your own still waiting to be written. We leave them in your capable hands. Take heart. You have wept and you have mourned. Listen closely, and you will hear the music drawing near. The time to laugh, the time to dance is fast approaching.